Columbia University
Contributions to Education

Teachers College Series

No. 466

AMS PRESS

NEW YORK

AN EXPERIMENTAL STUDY OF SPELLING METHODS

BY

CLAIRE TURNER ZYVE, Ph.D.

TEACHERS COLLEGE, COLUMBIA UNIVERSITY
CONTRIBUTIONS TO EDUCATION, No. 466

BUREAU OF PUBLICATIONS
Teachers College, Columbia University
NEW YORK CITY
1931

Library of Congress Cataloging in Publication Data

Zyve, Claire (Turner) 1895-
    An experimental study of spelling methods.

    Reprint of the 1931 ed., issued in series: Teachers
College, Columbia University. Contributions to edu-
cation, no. 466.
    Originally presented as the author's thesis, Columbia.
    Bibliography: p.
    1. English language--Orthography and spelling.
2. Spelling ability--Testing. I. Title. II. Series:
Columbia University. Teachers College. Contributions
to education, no. 466.
LB1574.Z9 1972   372.6'32   73-177606
ISBN 0-404-55466-0

Reprinted by Special Arrangement with Teachers
College Press, New York, New York

From the edition of 1931, New York
First AMS edition published in 1972
Manufactured in the United States

AMS PRESS, INC.
NEW YORK, N. Y.   10003

ACKNOWLEDGMENTS

I wish to acknowledge the advice and help unsparingly given to me during the completion of this study by the members of the dissertation committee: Professors Lois C. Mossman, Edwin H. Reeder, and Arthur I. Gates. I am also deeply indebted for friendly and critical assistance from Professors Milo B. Hillegas, J. Ralph McGaughy, Annie E. Moore, and Dr. Jean Betzner.

The collection of the experimental data was made possible through the coöperation of the following members of the Fox Meadow School staff: Miss Mary Roeder, Mrs. Lucile Noble, Miss Ruth MacArthur, Mrs. Gertrude Furey, Miss Ella Hagedorn, Miss Mary Urmston, Miss Beatrice Fleming, Miss Ethel Christensen, Miss Marjorie Knopf, Miss Helen Hultz, Miss Ruth Furlong, Miss Catherine Urell. I welcome this opportunity to make public acknowledgment of the contribution to the study which came from their careful teaching.

C. Z.

CONTENTS

AN EXPERIMENTAL STUDY OF
SPELLING METHODS

.   .   .

CHAPTER I

INTRODUCTION

The Problem

In spite of the evident interest in solving the problem of efficient and adequate teaching and learning of spelling words, any solution offered up to the present is far from satisfactory. The Department of Superintendence *Fourth Yearbook* [9, p. 171]* includes among "Suggested Problems for Further Research" this statement: "Additional investigations need to be made to determine the relative efficiency of different methods of teaching spelling."

This may seem surprising in the face of the continuous interest in the problem, as shown by the many articles published and the many investigations made. Watson [50, p. 7] reports the analysis of 339 separate publications relating to spelling from which her selected bibliography of 61 references was chosen; Horn [24] has taken 133 bibliographical references as the basis for his spelling "principles"; Tidyman [49] includes 187 articles and books in his bibliography; the chapter on spelling in Reed, *Psychology of the Elementary Subjects* [43] has a selected bibliography of 48 references; while Sister Irmina's annotated bibliography [26], the most recent comprehensive bibliography, has 296 titles. The selected bibliography of the present study on pages 82 to 84 includes only the articles and books on methods in elementary school spelling to which direct reference is made. These were chosen after an examination of 252 references dealing primarily with the methods of teaching or learning words, and 120 additional articles concerning grade lists, standards, and scales. However, in 84 of the articles dealing with method, the conclusions given are without the evidence of checked observation, or seem to be based on discussion or personal opinion; in the remaining 168 more or less

* Numbers in brackets refer to references in Bibliography, pp. 82 to 84.

I

carefully collected data, objectively and statistically interpreted, have been used. In many cases, in this latter group, the time for the reported investigation was short and the numbers used were few, with many uncontrolled factors operating.

The elements in method on which there have been divergent or uncertain points of view are well summarized by Horn [24], who supports his statement of the prevailing view by results of investigations made previous to the time of the writing of his article. Reed [43] in a later analysis of various problems pertaining to spelling method has included results of additional investigations. There is, however, some doubt among writers as to whether the statement of "principles" of spelling method based on the data published in 1919 [50, p. 359] is justified.

Problems in the Study of the Mastery of Spelling

There are two distinct problems involved in the study of the mastery of spelling: first, the choice of words to be taught, and second, the methods of teaching and learning the words after they have been selected. The present investigation deals with the second problem. It does not involve data or discussions on lists of words, tests, or grade standards, nor does it touch on the problem of the social uses of spelling and of the attitudes which should be developed toward it as an integral part of expression. Further, there are certain problems in method, such as the teaching of homonyms, or the value of rules and generalization groupings in the learning of words, on which no data are given. The attitude of the writer is not that the whole spelling problem is necessarily a matter of specific bond learning but that whatever the method of spelling teaching eventually evolved, there will always be need of isolated word presentation and study.

The problem, then, of the present study is to report and interpret the results of spelling teaching and learning so controlled as to give additional data on some of the problems in spelling method on which results previously published have been either conflicting or meagre. The factors which are considered here are teacher-directed study as compared with individual study; study of words solely from lists, as compared with the writing of words in sentences during study; the effect of home-work review as compared with the effect of teacher-directed review; comparison of the efficiency of the blackboard with that of a lantern projector for the presentation of words; the effect of emphasis on the form of the word before study by identification among similar forms, combined with more careful attention to the form of the word in the child's own writing; and the results from limiting the study of new words to four of the five days of the week, using the fifth day for systematic review. For convenience, the factors referred to as "the effect of emphasis on the form of the word before study by identification among similar forms" and "more careful attention to the form of the word in the child's own writing" are usually designated in the discussion as "other factors in form."

CHAPTER II

ANALYSIS OF PREVIOUS STUDIES PERTAINING TO THE POINTS INVESTIGATED

There is still disagreement or uncertainty among authorities and investigators on many points in spelling method. The present study, without offering final solutions, uses a method which includes factors concerning which there is some disagreement; on other factors, it submits additional data. This chapter consists of a summary of the most important investigations to date of the methods used in this investigation on which there is lack of uniformity in opinion and practice. Since the study is confined to the investigation of certain elements in teaching method, the summaries given will be only of investigations dealing directly with problems in method pertinent here. These include the test-study method, syllabication of words, time for spelling study, number of words to be taught per week, teacher-directed as compared with independent study, context as compared with list teaching, home- and teacher-directed review, visualization as an element in method, and methods of study and plans of work for the week.

Test-Study Plan and Study-Test Plan

An open question is that of the relative value of the test-study method versus the study-test method in spelling. The present investigation required the use of the test-study method for a valid comparison of results of the factors investigated. As shown in the analysis of the data of the present experiment in a later chapter, page 79, there is some reason to believe that the longer form of preliminary test is more practical for school use than the weekly shorter preliminary test. Aside from the expression of this opinion, however, there is no discussion of this problem in the present study.

With regard to the test-study plan versus the study-test plan, L. R. Kilzer reports in the *School Review* of September 1926 [30] an investigation which indicates that the test-study plan is superior in some respects to the study-test plan.

4

In the investigation of the test-study as opposed to the study-test plan in the teaching of spelling, Kilzer has collected data from 34 high schools in eight states, and has immediate-recall test scores of 1,000 pupils in Grade 9 and delayed-recall test scores of 777 of the same pupils tested five months later. To avoid overweighting results from the larger schools, not more than 76 pupils were included from any one school.

The method of investigation is reported in the following steps: Two lists of words, A and B, were chosen, each having 25 words equalized in frequency according to Horn's study, *The 10,000 Words Most Commonly Used in Writing*, and of the same difficulty of spelling according to Ayres' *Measuring Scale for Ability to Spell*. In schools 1 to 18, list A was used for the study-test method, and list B for the test-study method. This use was reversed in schools 19 to 34.

In the study-test plan each pupil was given a printed list of words. The teacher pronounced these words and the pupils were given 20 minutes to study without direction as to method. The 10 minutes used by the teacher in pronouncing the words brought the total amount of time to 35 minutes.

A second list of words was dictated a few days after the completion of the first list. The pupils exchanged papers and underlined all misspelled words, checking from printed lists. The words which had been misspelled were then underlined on other printed lists which were given to the pupils with instructions to study the underlined words for 10 minutes; again no specific study directions were made. The pupils who had all words correct did not study, but were tested with the group on the entire list at the close of the period. The amount of time used totaled 35 minutes.

Five months later 777 of the same 1,000 pupils in 30 of the 34 high schools participated in delayed-recall tests. A summary of the test for immediate-recall follows:

1. All words misunderstood were counted wrong.
2. One hundred and fifty-five papers were thrown out of the first 1,000 papers because pupils failed to underline misspelled words in Test-Study 1.
3. The test-study plan was superior in both groups of schools. In schools 1 to 18, the chances were 226 to 1 that the method was superior. In schools 19-34, the chances were 80 to 1 that the method was superior.
4. Test-study was significantly superior for the best spellers, and at least as good for the poorest spellers.

5. In Test-Study 2 after 10 minutes of study, there were only one-fifth as many cases of misspelling as in Test-Study 1.

Results for the delayed-recall test were as follows:

1. There were no significant differences between study-test and test-study methods for delayed-recall when five months had elapsed without drill. In 10 schools the study-test method was superior and in 20 schools the test-study method was superior, but in many cases the superiority was negligible.
2. There was no significant difference for either the best or the poorest spellers.
3. Errors made with the test-study method do not tend to persist to any greater extent than do errors made with the study-test method.

Kingsley [31, p. 129] experimented for two years with Grades 5 and 8 in two schools in Albany, New York, comparing the test-study and the study-test methods in spelling. He does not report the number of cases used and did not control the use of texts nor the methods of procedure and recitation. Kingsley gives a general summary of his results as follows:

1. Grades using test-study method show much better gains in class average.
2. The general average for the grades using the test-study method is somewhat higher than that of the grades using the study-test method.

Horn [24, pp. 60-61] definitely expresses his views of the pre-test in two statements: "Test all words before teaching," and "The resulting feeling of dissatisfaction of having missed the word, plus the concentrated attack on remedying the exact difficulty, more than outweighs any disadvantage rising from the initial misspelling."

Fred S. Breed [6, p. 301] comments on the pre-test as follows:

One of the arguments often urged against the test-study method is based on the theory of the persistence of the initial error. It is inadvisable to use a method that permits a pupil to get a wrong start on a word by misspelling. . . . Woody found that there was no significant tendency in the pre-test method to cause errors made in the first spelling of a word to persist. This same conclusion is supported by other investigators.

Devine and Hulten [10, p. 121] suggest a modified form of pre-testing in which children will be required to write only those words which they are reasonably sure of spelling correctly. They base their recommendation on an experiment with 38 fifth grade children in Marinette, Wisconsin. One group wrote all the words pronounced; the other, only the ones of which they were certain.

Group I missed 32.4 per cent of the words which they wrote; Group II did not attempt 68.7 per cent and missed 3.6 per cent of those they wrote. The authors point out the fact that Group I must have been writing many words of which they were not sure and that a modified form of the pre-test as suggested above would help develop a "spelling consciousness" on the part of the pupils.

Although the use of test-study versus study-test in the teaching of spelling cannot be a part of this investigation, the use of test-study, in the light of present-day investigation, seems to be a positive element in method.

SYLLABICATION OF WORDS

Whether or not words shall be divided into syllables during the teaching of spelling, has been another matter of considerable controversy. The tendency, as it is seen in opinions given and in studies made, is in the direction of conceding the probable value of syllabication. In the present investigation all words of more than one syllable were divided. Words were divided in the text in that part of the study in which Pearson and Suzzallo, *Essentials of Spelling* [42] was used; and in the phase using the blackboard and lantern slides each word was presented in both divided and undivided form.

The bulk of opinion and evidence in the following references is in favor of syllabication, although the evidence given is not entirely decisive. Jones[1] believes that syllabication is a hindrance to learning, while Wolfe and Breed [52] find the opposite to be true. The investigation of Wolfe and Breed was conducted for the purpose of testing words gained through use of syllabication as against undivided words. Their study was made in the elementary school of the University of Chicago, where 52 poor spellers at or below class median from Grades 4A, 5B, 5A, 6B, 7B, and 7A were selected. Two lists of 60 words each from the Ayres scale were taught to the two groups. Lists of words were dictated in sentences over a period of 15 days, with 20 minutes per day devoted to the work. Five steps were included in the method: pronunciation and development of meaning; oral and written spelling by the pupils; study; review of previous day's lesson; test. The words were printed and presented on tag board, syllabified or

[1] "Sliced Elephants," an advertising pamphlet for *Jones Speller*. Hall and McCreary Company, Chicago (about 1925).

undivided, according to the group, and exposed for two minutes. Five new words were taught each day. These were included in the sentences dictated. In the results of the test termed the final test, administered immediately after all words had been taught, there was evidence of superiority of syllabication. This superiority was more noticeable with the younger than with the older pupils. In another test, given 23 days after the final test, there were indications, though less marked, that syllabication was attended with a slightly better result. In this case, also, the superiority of syllabication was more marked with the younger than with the older pupils, although, on the whole, in the classes tested, syllabication seemed to produce slightly better results than non-division of words.

The attitude of spelling-text compilers toward syllabication has been studied by Greene [19, p. 208], who found from an examination of 61 spelling texts published between 1800 and 1917 the attitude as determined by practice to be as follows: in favor of syllabication only, 38.3 per cent; syllabication, diacritics, accents, 20 per cent; syllabication and accents, 20 per cent; and no division, 21.7 per cent. Twelve textbooks published since 1907 show: syllabication only, 33.3 per cent; syllabication, diacritics, accents, 8.3 per cent; syllabication, accents, 16.7 per cent; and no division, 41.7 per cent. An examination of 67 courses of study shows no consensus as to the form in which words should be presented.

Greene [19] also reports that data from 41 pupils (Grades 4, 5, and 6 at the University Elementary School, University of Iowa), over a period of 13 days, using words divided into syllables during one week and using words in units the next, show a slight superiority in favor of the syllabified form of the word. Individual spelling was used, and the spelling words were equated in difficulty. Words were paired into two lists on the basis of the number of misspellings, after which each list was prepared in syllabified and unit form. The method was, in general, similar to that set forth in the *Eighteenth Yearbook* of the National Society for the Study of Education [24, p. 72]. Each class was divided into two groups approximately equal in ability. Each studied a list of 25 words for seven days, the time including 40 minutes for study outside the testing time, with a delayed-recall test two weeks later, followed by the second test of 10 words for the second period. The author concludes that teaching the word in the syllabified form is the slightly superior method, but, in the largest difference between results obtained, the probable error of the difference is equal to more than half the difference. Thus there is no statistical surety that the difference in results is due to method. On the surface, it appears that the syllabified form of a word is slightly superior for earlier presentation in the lower grades, and also in the case of delayed-recall. Greene is not sure, however, that this difference is not due to other factors than the methods themselves.

Heilman [22] carried on an investigation in 1919 among 73 children in Grades 4, 5, and 7 of the elementary school of Colorado State Teachers College. The children of each grade were divided into two equal groups by the teacher of the grade. One hundred words were used for each grade, over a period of 35 school days, 20 of which were given to learning and testing. The difference found was not in the initial and the final tests, for no initial test was given. This psychologist concludes that in learning to spell a syllabized word the effect of the learning may be retained longer than when the word is unsyllabized, and this advantage may not appear until the word is relearned. It is also probable that teaching the children to syllabize their words in spelling gives them a better method of learning to spell strange words, which would become permanent acquisitions. As Heilman says,

When asked to spell a strange word of considerable length, all of us find it advantageous to syllabize the word. In general the syllabized form of the word promotes the learning process in spelling.

Stress on the syllabification of words is an important element in learning to spell, according to Horn [24, p. 66], who believes this is particularly true when the syllables are pronounced. Watson [50, p. 359], in speaking of the length of the word, says:

Studies cited [15] have indicated that length appears to be the most potent factor inherent within the word itself as affecting its spelling difficulty. The implication for teaching method seems to be that attention should be directed to units within long words, preferably to syllables.

Watson [50, p. 363] continues her discussion by saying:

Gates has emphasized most consistently and clearly the fundamental distinction between inappropriate and too phonetic analyses of words, and the highly recommended sounding of syllable-units and association therewith of corresponding visual-graphic forms.

Watson believes further that careful articulation of the word is of great importance, and that phonic training is sometimes the means of correcting the spelling.

The perception span is from three to five distinct objects, says Tidyman [49, p. 35], and therefore the syllable is important in learning to spell since it at once divides the word into a number of perceivable units, at the same time making possible a clear, definite, detailed picture of the letters.

Gates [17, p. 68] comments as follows:

. . . in many cases the spelling was correctly and often rapidly made in the case of familiar words or in the case of short words. Usually the successful spelling came to an abrupt halt when a new word or one exceeding a particular length was encountered. . . . It is probable that the type of attack indicated the way in which the words were observed. If they were observed as wholes, the spelling was usually correct up to a certain length beyond which the pupil was unable to proceed effectively. He might try to spell letter by letter, or approximate the whole, or try it by parts, now one way now another, but unless the significant details of the word had been observed specifically, a correct spelling would seldom result. . . . What was needed was a method of observing a word as a group of parts, each of which is not too minute and not too complex to handle and which enables him to perceive significant portions clearly.

And again [16, p. 80]—

syllabification is desirable. . . . The analysis should be made in terms of syllables, not letters, or phonetic elements. The pupils should learn to spell (recall) as they study, i.e., syllable by syllable, not letter by letter. . . .

Hollingworth's study [23, p. 42] to determine the most difficult sections of words presents the following findings: Of 102 errors in spelling of 11 polysyllabic words, 52 errors were on the intermediate syllable, 19 on the initial syllable, and 31 on the ultimate syllable. Twenty-seven dissyllabic words gave 60 errors on the ultimate and 37 on the initial syllable. The implication for pedagogy here seems to be that stress should be placed on intermediate and final syllables in the teaching of new words, as the initial element tends to take care of itself.

Watson [50, p. 358] cites a study reported by Brandenburg [5] showing that length of words is not the important factor which it is sometimes considered to be, since in one and one-half million words observed for possible misspellings, of the 19 words most misspelled only one has as many as five syllables and only two as many as eleven letters.

Investigation and opinion indicate that there is value in syllabication. They would seem to imply that it would be bad usage for the child to see the word only in divided form, since its usage in reading or writing will always be as a unit. In the present study the words were always first presented as a unit and then followed by the division into syllables, this presentation again being followed by the words written as a unit. Whether or not this point is important enough for a spelling text to have its lists printed in both divided and undivided form is a question which cannot be answered without further investigation.

Amount of Time to Be Allotted per Week for Spelling Study

There is fair agreement as to the amount of school time per week which should be devoted to spelling study. Throughout the present study the time used was 15 minutes a day, five days a week. An analysis of the data in Chapter V, however, seems to indicate that efficiency in method may make it possible to redistribute this time to include review.

Ayers reports the time devoted to spelling in 49 large cities in 1924 [29, p. 139] as follows:

Grade	Minutes per Week
1	39
2	82
3	87
4	85
5	82
6	78
7	72
8	73
Average	75

while the total minutes per week allotted to spelling in grades 1 to 8 in elementary schools for the past four decades is as follows:

Year	No. of Minutes
1888	832
1904	497
1914	704
1924	598

Dr. Horn [24, p. 59] says that if spelling is taught daily the spelling periods should not be more than 15 minutes in length.

He quotes from a study made by Lauterbach, "Status of Spelling in 80 Cities" (an unpublished study of the University of Iowa), according to which in 1914 the median time for 80 cities was 50 minutes per week in Grade 1, and 75 minutes in Grades 2 through 9. Dr. Horn continues his discussion by saying that the amount of time spent on spelling should certainly not exceed 75 minutes per week, including both study and recitation.

Stigler [46, p. 25], in his article on "Better Spelling and Less Drill," says, "Children of to-day spell better than did children of our grandfathers. . . . the time devoted to the study of spelling in the primary grades has been gradually reduced from 74 per cent of the school day to less than 8 per cent."

That the amount of time in itself is not an index of sure results has been pointed out by Reed [43, p. 232] in reporting Nifenecker's study:

There is not a consistent relationship between efficiency in spelling and the amount of time devoted to it in class. In a study reported by Nifenecker on 5,260 fifth grade children in the city of New York the highest score, 87.6, came with 70 minutes per week while the next highest, 74.3, was achieved with 100 minutes a week. The lowest score, 21.7, was also with 70 minutes per week, while the next to the lowest, 31.7, was obtained with 100 minutes per week. The highest number of minutes per week was 120, which in three cases brought scores of 65.9, 44.7, and 43.5.

Here, as Reed points out, there is no guarantee that 120 minutes include more repetitions than 70 minutes. The efficacy of the repetitions is determined by their intensity, and by the purpose of the learner, and so on.

The Number of Words to Be Taught

This present belief that a reasonable amount of time for spelling recitation and drill is a fifteen-minute period every day in the week has been directly conditioned not only by improved methods of teaching but by the results of research on the total number of words which should be taught. , As the lists of words in the elementary school courses of study have decreased in number from 10,000 or 15,000 [45, p. 383] to about 4,000, with a probable further reduction with additional research, the amount of time necessary for teaching them has of course also been decreased. Formerly, it was not unusual to find 20 words a day given for the spelling assignment; now 15 or 20 words are considered a reasonable allotment for the week's work.

It is the belief of Horn [24, p. 59] that it is impossible to advise finally concerning the number of words to be taught per lesson without knowing the conditions. His conclusions, based on two preliminary experiments, are that a test should be given on a large number of words at one time (25 to 50 according to the grade) and then as many periods should be used as are necessary for each pupil to learn the words which he has missed.

In the present investigation, 16 new words were taught each week, following an initial test of 80 words which covered the advance words for five weeks.

TEACHER-DIRECTED AND INDEPENDENT STUDY

The present study offers data on the problem of teacher-directed and independent study. This was one of the earliest problems in spelling method receiving experimental attention, and is still, due to the rise of interest in individual instruction, a problem on which there is wide divergence of points of view.

An early investigation conducted to discover the comparative results from teacher-directed study and independent study of spelling was that conducted by Henry Carr Pearson in the Horace Mann School and reported in the *Teachers College Record* of January 1912 [41]. In Pearson's first experiment two rooms each of Grades 4, 5, and 6 were paired on their ability to spell 25 words in dictated sentences. Half the rooms were taught by class study in five fifteen-minute periods with no outside time allowed. The remaining grades studied independently for 15 minutes per day with unlimited outside time. After 10 days a final test was given and progress was measured in the amount of decrease in errors; this decrease was greater in the case of the independent study with outside time given to the work.

The remainder of the year was devoted to an experiment to determine whether class-directed study by the teacher resulted in better independent study habits. The same method was used throughout the experimental period from November to May. After this period 10 words were given to the pupils to be studied independently in two lessons. The group which had spent the year in independent study again had better results, though not so great in proportion as at the end of the first experiment.

A second experiment with Grades 3 and 7, with a time limit for the daily lesson of 20 minutes and no outside time, followed with these results:

| | | AVERAGE DECREASE PER PUPIL ERRORS | |
GRADE	No. OF PUPILS	Class Study	Individual Study
3 29		5.24	...
3 27		...	4.40
7 24		4.46	...
7 26		...	4.04

Here the class-study method was more effective when measured in decrease of errors.

To eliminate teacher effect was the purpose of the third experiment which followed these two. It included Grades 4, 5, 6, and 7, with each teacher presenting both methods to the same children. The interval before the final test was increased from 10 to 24 days, the individual study recitation period was made 18 minutes, and the class-study period was made 15 minutes. The number of words varied in the different grades from 20 in Grade 3 to 32 in Grade 7, the words being taught in four different periods. Here again was a marked superiority in the results obtained from class study:

| | AVERAGE DECREASE PER PUPIL | |
GRADE	Individual Study	Class Study
4 .... 2.63		5.95
5 .... 4.15		9.15
6 .... 5.56		9.56
7 .... 6.65		9.10

| AVERAGE DECREASE PER GRADE ERRORS | |
Individual Study	Class Study
4.74	8.44

In the fourth of Pearson's experiments the time for independent study was increased to 25 minutes while the class study was kept at 15 minutes. The teachers using the independent study plan followed this procedure at the beginning of the period:

1. Wrote words on board.
2. Pronounced word.
3. Pointed out special difficulties.
4. Had pupils study 15 minutes.
5. Used five minutes in dictation testing.

In this experiment the class-study method was slightly superior in Grade 6 and the independent method superior in Grade 4.

Mr. Pearson's conclusions are that, with time constant, class study gives better results.

In the *Pedagogical Seminary* of June 1914, Martha Fulton [12] reports an experiment conducted with 28 children in Grade 4B to measure the efficiency of individual- and teacher-directed drill. She taught 100 words in 10 days employing the following method of teaching each word:

1. Wrote word on board.
2. Explained meaning of word.
3. Had children use word in sentence.
4. Had children write word 10 times repeating out loud.
5. Emphasized by tone or colored chalk the difficult parts of the word.

Following this procedure another group of 100 words was given to the children to study with no direction except to "study the lesson." The children were tested every day and the next lesson was assigned. Results of the study are given in the tabulation below:

	WITH DRILL	THREE WEEKS LATER	WITHOUT DRILL	TWO WEEKS LATER
Average grades	98	96	73	68
Average deviation	1.9	3.4	11.2	11.8

In this case the number of children tested is small and the comparative difficulty of the two groups of 100 words not assured. The author does not take into account the carry-over in method of study from the directed study which came first, when she says no help was given in independent study.

E. E. Keener reports in the *Journal of Educational Method* for September 1926 [28] a comparison of the group and individual methods of teaching spelling used in Chicago public schools in 1924-1925. In this study 976 paired pupils in Grades 2 through 8 were taught 100 words in five weeks' time with five fifteen-minute periods per week. The pupils in half the rooms were taught by the teacher, and those in the other half studied individually.

These were the plans used in the teacher-directed study:

1. Write the word on the board.
2. Pronounce, emphasizing syllables.
3. Explain the meaning.
4. Use in a sentence or have pupils do so.
5. Spell orally and note division into syllables.
6. Spell orally in concert with the pupils.
7. Call attention to difficult parts.

8. Erase and have pupils write.
9. Spell orally as pupils check written word.
10. Repeat for all four words.
11. Test. Have children exchange papers and mark errors.
12. Have children keep individual lists of words missed.
13. If word is difficult repeat steps 1-9.
14. Direct pupils in study of words misspelled.
15. Give test on Friday of 20 words for week and 20 words of previous week.

The plans used in the individual study were as follows:

1. On Friday test pupils with the 20 words for the following week.
2. Have pupils correct and make lists of words missed.
3. Check each child's list. If he has perfect paper excuse him from study but not from test at end of week.
4. Monday to Friday have each pupil study his individual list until he can spell every word.
5. Give individual help in room where needed.
6. Pupils should be taught proper method of study. Give instruction as follows:
   (*a*) Pronounce word in whisper. Be sure each syllable is sounded.
   (*b*) Learn meaning of word and use in sentence.
   (*c*) Cover and pronounce, trying to see each syllable. Spell word in a whisper.
   (*d*) Look at word and be sure you spelled it correctly.
   (*e*) Cover word and write it on a piece of paper.
   (*f*) Compare with book. Be sure you have written it correctly.
   (*g*) Repeat (*a*)-(*f*) until you are sure you can spell word correctly.
7. On Friday give a test on entire 20 words for week, 20 of previous week, and 20 of next week.
8. Each pupil's task for next week is to learn words misspelled in this test.
9. Each pupil should keep individual list of words missed in written work in other subjects.

With a total of 488 pairs of pupils, the average number of words learned when measured by subtracting initial and final scores on 100 words was 18.3, and the average number learned by the individual method was 19.0. This gave a difference of .7 of a word in favor of individual study. There follows a partial summary of the results of Keener's investigation:

1. With all grades compared, individual study is slightly superior to group instruction.
2. Indications were that group instruction secured better results in Grades 2 and 3.
3. With pupils grouped on the basis of initial spelling ability, individual study was better in all groups except those scoring below 30 per cent (2 pairs in second grade).

4. The individual method was slightly superior where the two methods were taught by the same teacher.
5. Teachers favored the individual method.
6. About 12 per cent of the pupils were excused from the study of spelling for initial perfect scores.

On 100 words, scores in per cent on the initial test and average improvement in the number of words are given in the following tabulation:

COMPARISON OF IMPROVEMENT IN SPELLING ABILITY UNDER GROUP AND INDIVIDUAL INSTRUCTION

Per Cent on Initial Test	No. of Pairs	Av. Improvement	
		Group Study	Individual Study
90	137	6.0	6.4
80	163	12.9	13.3
70	73	22.0	22.5
60	50	29.1	30.1
50	27	37.0	41.0
40	22	48.0	49.7
30	14	52.8	56.4
Below 30	2	72.0	40.0

In the study of Keener's described above, the initial number of words wrong was not given by grades, which makes it impossible to determine whether the learning load was greater in one grade than in another. The plan for individual study would seem to make these results include the effect of review, more than does the group method, for in the individual-study plan the child *studied* the following week the words missed the previous two weeks, as well as the words missed during the current week. The only provision made for review study in the group plan was following the Friday test of 40 words, and as only 15 minutes were allowed, the time for review study must necessarily have been very short.

Woody [53, p. 160] conducted an experiment in 1924-1925 in Grades 6, 7, and 8 in the public schools of Adrian, Michigan, to evaluate the effect of what he describes as the "traditional" method of teaching in comparison with a variation of the "test and study" method upon the temporary and permanent mastery of the spelling of given lists of 100 words, and upon the number and persistency of errors. He enumerates the following points as representing the outstanding differences between the control and the experimental methods of teaching spelling:

OUTSTANDING DIFFERENCES BETWEEN THE TWO
METHODS OF TEACHING SPELLING

METHOD I: CONTROL	METHOD II: EXPERIMENTAL
1. Five new and 5 review words taught daily.	1. Twenty words per week given on first day.
2. Children study words before being tested.	2. Children tested on words before studying them.
3. Teacher directs all children in study of each word.	3. Children study only words missed on tests.
4. All children must study the words assigned.	4. Children spelling correctly all words on tests are excused from study of words.
5. Teacher largely controls formation of habits of study.	5. Pupils must assume greater amount of responsibility in formation of study habits.
6. Children tested on 10 words of daily assignment for 4 days of week and on 20 words assigned for the week on Friday.	6. Children tested on 20 new words per week on Monday, Wednesday, and Friday, and on 20 words of previous week on Wednesday and Friday.
7. Children tested on each word 3 different times.	7. Children tested on each word 5 different times.
8. Some testing of spelling each day of the week.	8. No testing of spelling on 2 days of the week.

The conclusions of this study are based upon results from paired groups with perfect attendance, which numbered 40; and those with not more than two days of absence, numbering 70. The pairs were matched on the basis of grade, sex, attendance, approximate age, mental ability, achievement on the initial test, and educational and social environment. Woody's conclusions are that there is no significant difference in results of the control and the experimental methods of teaching as used in the experiment, either in the total number of errors, in the total number of different errors, or in the persistence of errors from the first tests to later tests.

As will be readily seen, the results of these studies on the efficacy of teacher-directed drill are not in agreement. Pearson and Fulton find it to have a positive effect as compared with individual study, Keener believes individual study is more efficient, while Woody finds no significant difference in the methods as he used them. The problem of the efficacy of teacher-directed drill is one of those on which data are submitted in Chapter IV of the present study.

Context and List Teaching

A report of experimentation on the effect of including a certain amount of context teaching in the learning of words is also included in the present study. This is another problem in spelling method on which several investigations have been made. Most of these have compared the accuracy of the use of words in context or lists, or the learning of words entirely in context or in list settings. The present study compares word-learning in lists, with a compromise method of part isolated study and part contextual use.

One study of misspelling in context is that of Lester's [34, p. 117], who summarizes the work of various investigations on the relative amount of misspellings in written composition as follows:

Amount of Misspellings in Written Composition According to Various Investigators

Investigator	No. of Students Whose Work Was Investigated	Location	Age or Scholastic Standing	No. of Words Misspelled for Every 100 Written
Bailey	171	Yale Univ. Wis.	Seniors and juniors	.240
Brandenburg	96	Ill., Md., Iowa, S. D.	Grades 2-8	.315
Jones	1,050	S. D.	Grades 2-8	.336
Brandenburg	96	Purdue Univ.	All 4 classes	.55
Lester	2,414	All states	Candidates for college	1.02
Cornman	....	Phila.	Grades 2-8	2.30
Cook and O'Shea	2	Wis.	Grade 8	7.17

Tidyman and Brown [48, p. 212] quote several investigators who have made studies of the problem of context spelling. Among these is Cornman, who concludes that there is little if any transfer from column to dictation exercises [7, p. 44]. Wallin's findings contradict Cornman's conclusions, showing that the loss in transfer does not amount to over two words in a hundred, while the findings of Cook and O'Shea show the loss to be about 5 per cent. Wallin, Cook and O'Shea, in their investigations, did not eliminate the words which the children knew before teaching. Tidyman and

Brown found, however, that if these words were eliminated the loss in transfer from column to dictation spelling was 11 per cent.

In an effort to determine whether children spell equally well in column and context spelling, R. V. Hunkins [25] reports an experiment in 1919, which was carried out in Hot Springs, South Dakota. The study was made with 165 children from Grades 3 through 8. Lists of 20 words were taken from the Ayres Scale for each grade. Grade 8 used 10 words. The author arranged the grade lists of selected words into paragraph story form, suitable for the grade intended. The story was dictated and was then followed by a repetition of the words given in a dictated list. The arithmetic mean for the mean differences in the results favored the column test by 10.9 per cent. Better scores on the column test were made by 69.7 per cent of the children. Although this experiment does not relate directly to method, it suggests the necessity for some context teaching in method, since use in context is the situation offering most difficulty in the spelling of words.

A study to determine spelling difficulty in context form was made by Paul McKee [36] in 1921, and was carried out with 401 seventh grade pupils attending the public schools of Iowa. McKee used in this study 10 seventh grade words of varying difficulty, selected from the Buckingham Extension of the Ayres Spelling Scale. These words were made into two tests, one a column-form test and the other a paragraph-form test, the latter consisting of a business letter in which the 10 words were used. The paragraph test was dictated to the 401 seventh grade pupils and was immediately followed by the column-form test. The results of McKee's study show that pupils spell better and with greater accuracy in column form than in paragraph form. This fact was determined by comparing the percentage of accuracy secured on the paragraph test. The loss of transfer was computed; in connection with the computation McKee states the following facts:

> Loss of transfer did not occur in the case of every word.
> There was a greater loss in transfer for the more difficult word as determined by the Ayres scale.
> Some pupils spelled with greater accuracy in paragraph form than in column form.
> Many pupils exhibited no loss in transfer whatever.
> Many pupils used a different form of misspelling in context form than in column form.

A study having somewhat the same conclusions as that made by Hunkins is reported in the *Journal of Educational Research*, April 1922, by Hawley and Gallup [21]. This study was conducted to discover if the sentence method of teaching spelling equalized the deficiency in spelling context. The investigation was carried on in two Rochester, New York, schools, in which the children were from English-speaking homes. The grades used were Grades 3 through 8, inclusive, making a total of 1,100 pupils, who were taught by 32 teachers. Rooms of corresponding grade in the two schools were used throughout the experiment, one teaching the words in lists, the other in sentences. The study extended through 30 lessons. A test was given at the end of each 10 lessons. The lessons were conducted daily and were 15 minutes in length, with the exception of the lessons in the 3rd grade, where the period was 20 minutes long. An initial test of 25 words to determine the spelling ability of the groups was made for each grade by the principal. After these lists were given in sentences, the test words were pronounced in lists. All lists of words taught were grade lists taken from Pearson. After the first three tests, each of which was given following 10 lessons, a fourth test covering all the words given up to that point was made. Each day's results were tested by one group's writing the words in lists and a corresponding group's writing them in sentences.

The results are presented in the tabulation on page 22. The authors' conclusions are as follows:

1. The ability of a child to use spelling words in sentences is lower than in lists both with unfamiliar and with familiar words.
2. Teaching words through use in sentences rather than in lists does not equalize this ability to use words in lists and in sentences.
3. The pupils taught by the list method made slightly superior gains measured in differences between the initial ability tests and Test IV than did the pupils taught by context.

In this study initial tests were not given on the words taught, so the measure of progress could not be made in gains. Perhaps it is true that the difficulty of the words in the initial test, by which ability was roughly measured, may not have been the same as that of the words in the lists taught. No report is made of the way in which the other factors in method were controlled, and the assumption is made that a twenty-five word test selected by the principal is a true measure of ability. This study seems

     An Experimental Study of Spelling Methods

to offer conclusive evidence only in proving that accuracy in use of words is lower in sentences than in lists.

Another study concerned with the relative efficiency of the column and context forms of teaching was reported by Dr. Paul McKee in 1927 [37]. Five hundred seventh grade pupils in public schools in Iowa and Minnesota were used for this study.

Dr. McKee's investigation included three experiments, each of which covered the teaching of eight lessons. The pupils were arranged in two groups of equal spelling ability. In the first ex-

RESULTS OF TEACHING WORDS BY LIST AND BY CONTEXT METHODS

| | GRADE 3 | | | | GRADES 5 AND 6 | | | | GRADES 4 TO 8, INCLUSIVE | | | |
| | TEST I | | TEST IV | | TEST I | | TEST IV | | TEST I | | TEST IV | |
	List	Context	List	Context	List	Context	List	Context	List	Context	List	Context
TAUGHT BY LISTS												
No. pupils	81	81	82	87	202	201	203	205	412	412	418	420
Per cent correct	77.7	69.2	88.7	86.5	59.6	55.6	89.9	86.8	68.4	65.0	90.5	89.2
TAUGHT BY CONTEXT												
No. pupils	56	56	57	57	165	166	171	171	458	457	456	456
Per cent correct	62.3	55.0	88.1	83.4	63.5	59.2	89.8	88.8	70.8	65.8	89.7	88.4

periment, conducted to discover the relative efficiency of learning words in columns and in phrases, Group A studied the words in column form, and was tested during the teaching process by column-form tests. At the same time, Group B studied the words in phrases, with tests in phrase form. During the teaching of the last four lessons the groups were shifted. The same procedure was followed in the second experiment, with the words studied in columns and in sentences. A similar plan was used in the third experiment, with words presented in columns and in paragraphs. Delayed-recall tests were given nine weeks after the teaching of a particular lesson, both in column form and in the type of context form that was used in the teaching.

In the immediate-recall tests the group which used the words in columns showed greater relative improvement than the group which used the words in either phrases or paragraphs. The column-sentence experiment showed the column group to be only slightly superior to the sentence group. In the delayed-recall tests the results from all three experiments found the column group significantly superior.

The group which used the phrase form during the teaching process showed less ability to transfer previously studied words than did the group using the column method. The column-phrase experiment showed the ability to transfer words previously studied into new context forms.

As in the Hawley-Gallup experiment, this series of experiments seems to indicate that context exercises are not an efficient tool for increasing efficiency in spelling in context form. However, since context spelling presents difficulty, it would seem wise to use some form of context teaching as part of the spelling method to test the sure acquisition of the word. This contextual use may be combined with the study of the word as an isolated problem.

To find out if pupils know the meanings of words tested in context better than they do those tested in column form, is the purpose which H. W. Distad and Eva M. Davis [11] give for their study reported in 1929. For this experiment, 383 pupils were used, including pupils from eight high fifth grades, and six low fifth grades in several Atlanta and Houston public schools. As a first step in the study, two tests of equal spelling and vocabulary difficulty were constructed, with satisfactory reliability.

The experiment continued through four weeks, and during each week the group was taught 20 of the 80 words. On each Friday a vocabulary test was given in which the particular meaning used in teaching the word was tested. There were four groups of children, with an average of 95 children in each group, half of whom were high and half low fifth grade pupils. The procedure used was rotated in the groups, each one starting with a different week's work; in two of the four weeks the procedure was the same, with the exception of the words taught. The procedure for the week was as follows [11, p. 356]: Monday, the teacher wrote the word on the board, pronounced it, read *a sentence using the word*, and gave a list test following the presentation of all the words; Tuesday, the children studied individually the words missed; Wednesday, the teacher gave a test and corrected the list to discover the words to be studied on Thursday; Thursday, the same procedure was followed as on Tuesday; Friday, the same procedure was followed as on Wednesday. After the test on the 20 words, the vocabulary test was given on the same 20 words.

During the other two weeks of the period, the procedure was the same except that on Monday the presentation of the words was followed by the sentence-dictation test in which the words of the week were used. The procedure was the same throughout the week with the exception of Friday, when words were given in the repeated sentence-dictation test, which was also followed by the dictation test.

The authors do not give all the possible interesting results in the learning of the words under the two methods. They find all the differences on the vocabulary test in both immediate- and delayed-recall significantly in favor of the sentence-dictation method. They point out that words difficult to spell were purposely chosen. This difficulty in spelling probably carries over to difficulty in meaning for fifth grade pupils; thus the study shows the superiority of sentence-dictation spelling over column-dictation in the teaching of word meanings.

Since the first children had the words in oral context on Monday, the experiment offers a comparison of teaching word meanings in oral and dictated context.

Distad and Davis [11, p. 352], in commenting on studies comparing efficiency of column or list spelling with context spelling, say that these studies show a loss in efficiency through transfer.

That is, when the same words are presented in both column and context forms, the percentage of correct spelling is greater with the former than with the latter method. Further, it appears that pupils who study or are tested on words in column form are at no disadvantage when the words appear in new context form. For example, Winch [51, p. 99] found that pupils who studied words in column form possessed greater ability to transfer these words into cursive dictation than did pupils who studied the same words in context form. . . . Hawley and Gallup conclude from the results of their experiment: "In general the loss in spelling ability when pupils write in context cannot be prevented any more effectively by using a sentence method than it can by using the list method."

McKee [37, pp. 347-48], in discussing the same matter, says that pupils who studied and were tested by the column-form method were as efficient as or more efficient than pupils who studied and were tested by the phrase, sentence, or paragraph methods when words were presented in new context forms.

The results of an experiment which compared the validity of oral-recall, written-recall, and multiple-choice types of tests as means of indicating the words which pupils cannot spell, are reported by Guiler [20] in the *Journal of Educational Research* for October 1929. In Guiler's oral-recall test the word was first pronounced by the examiner and used in a meaningful sentence, and then spelled by the pupil on paper prepared for the purpose. In the written-recall type of test, each word in its most frequently misspelled form appeared in parentheses as a regular part of a meaningful sentence. The learner was directed to write the correct spelling of each misspelled word in the blank within the parentheses at the end of each line. In the multiple-choice type of test each sentence had four spellings of some particular word, in parentheses, as a regular part of a meaningful sentence. One of these spellings was correct, the other three incorrect. The misspellings were those most frequently found. The pupil underscored the word which he considered correct.

The data of this study come from 781 students from the seventh grade through the first year of college. All three methods were tried on 699 students; two methods, oral-recall and written-recall, were used with 82 additional students. The study involves 117,150 running words. Guiler gave the same list of 50 words to 380 students in their order of written-recall, oral-recall, and multiple-choice. The investigator then varied the order in which the tests were given to find the effect of precedence in giving the tests.

Guiler's investigation is summarized under these points:

1. Written-recall is on the whole the most effective of the three methods under investigation in detecting lack of word mastery. Multiple-choice is the least effective.
2. There does not seem to be any best method of testing spelling for all students. While written-response is found to be the most effective for the greatest number of students, oral-recall is the most effective for other students and multiple-choice for still others.
3. A composite test score derived from the tests used in the study is more reliable than a single test score.
4. The order in which the tests are given exerts a marked influence on the results. This influence seems to be due to practice effect.
5. Students with a high order of spelling ability exhibit far less varia-

tion in scores obtained from the three methods of testing than do students with a low order of spelling ability.

There was evidently practice effect in the test which was given second place but written-recall detected more errors than did oral-recall. Since oral-recall is less efficient in indicating errors, and since with most methods it is the form of test used in the preliminary test, it would seem that there has been unnecessary perturbation regarding the question of a child's studying words other than those missed on the initial test.

Home Study and Teacher-Directed Review

Another factor investigated and reported in the present investigation is the effect of study given to the spelling of words in addition to that given during the class time of the first week. This may be done, either by home work which means additional time given to individual study on the specific difficulties of a child or the class, or by teacher-directed review.

The home-work review method meant the addition of approximately one half-hour a week to the seventy-five minutes of class time used. In the present study the effects of this additional half-hour was measured in combination with four varying methods of class work. Pearson [41] measured the effect of unlimited outside time in combination with independent study of words and found that it equalized the poorer results which independent study had given in comparison with class-directed study when time was limited. As will be seen in a later chapter, very much the same result was obtained in the present study. Nifenecker's study [40], already referred to, does not indicate a positive relationship between time per week and results.

The teacher-directed review in the present instance consisted of teaching, on Tuesday and Thursday of the week following the first presentation of words, the words missed by the class on the preceding Friday's test, and measuring the effect of the amount of re-teaching during the intervening time. The present study does not attempt to solve the question of recurring reviews. How often they should come, their form, how long they should continue in the case of spelling are problems for other researches. Much of the general psychology of repetitions would of course apply here.

Reed [43, p. 6] found that an hour's work in addition problems yielded a gain of 37 per cent in speed when distributed in the form of one sitting a day for three days as against 12 per cent when the hour's practice was all done in one sitting. He says,

Other experiments seem to justify the assumption that the more distributed repetitions are, the more effective they are, remembering that the nature of the subject matter, the amount of the distribution and the amount of practice at one sitting condition results.

He continues, maintaining that distribution gives

less fatigue, more first impressions, and gives the learner the benefit of increased strength in neurones which have had their nutrition stimulated by exercise.

Gates [16, p. 287] says, in speaking of distribution of reviews:

. . . Evidence . . . indicates that one should overlearn somewhat at the beginning and leave the remainder of the overlearnings to reviews at constantly increasing intervals.

He suggests that the first review be a thorough one, and occur after 48 hours; the next, shorter, a week later; the next, three weeks later; the next, two months later; others at intervals of six months or more.

EMPHASIS ON VISUALIZATION

The present study also reports the result of experiments on increased attention to the visual form of the word, made possible by presenting the word on lantern slides, by identifying the word among similar but unlike forms, and by observing the form of the word in the subject's own writing. Mention of the necessity for attention to visual analysis of a word has been made by several writers on the subject. A suggestion for better habits of visualization as an element in better method in spelling, has been given by Dr. A. I. Gates and Esther Hemke Chase who report on studies of deaf children's spelling in the *Journal of Educational Psychology* of May 1926 [18]. This report includes the results of a study of the reading and spelling abilities of 45 children in the Institution for the Improvement of Instruction of Deaf Mutes in New York City. The authors say [p. 290]:

Before giving the tests of spelling ability the achievements of the pupils in reading were ascertained since there are good reasons for believing that absolute spelling ability is greatly influenced by the level of ability and amount of experience in reading.

The Burgess reading test was given [18, pp. 290-91] with results as tabulated below:

INSTITUTION GRADE	APPROX. SCHOOL GRADE	NO. OF PUPILS	AV. CHRON. AGE	AV. READING AGE	AV. READING GRADE
7B 3B		12	13.6	....	...
8B 4B		11	14.2	8.2	2.5
9B 5B		9	16.4	8.5	2.8
10B 8B		13	18.1	10.0	3.5

This was followed by a spelling test of 36 words from the Ayres-Buckingham Scale. The list comprised nine groups of three words, each of the same length, beginning with 2-letter words and culminating with 11-letter words. By translating the raw scores into the chronological age of normal children who average the same score the following average spelling ages were obtained [18, pp. 292-93]:

AV. ACTUAL AGE OF DEAF	AV. SPELLING AGE	SPELLING AGE NORMAL CHILDREN OF SAME READING ABILITY	SUPERIORITY IN YEARS OF DEAF
13.6 .... 11.2		6.9	4.3
14.2 .... 11.6		8.1	3.5
16.4 .... 12.6		8.4	4.2
18.1 .... 13.0		9.4	3.6

The authors point out that, compared to their ability in reading, the deaf pupils' spelling achievements are very high. The spelling of the deaf, thus computed, is about 150 per cent that of the normal child.

A spelling recognition test was devised as a further means of testing the spelling abilities of the deaf pupils. It consisted of 36 words, varying in length and difficulty, each presented with four misspellings. The task for the pupil was to underline the correct word. When compared with normal pupils of the same reading ability the differences in favor of the deaf in years were:

DEAF GROUP GRADE	DIFF. IN FAVOR OF DEAF IN YEARS
7B	2.5
8B	2.7
9B	4.3
11B	5.2

Handicaps caused by difference in ability in lip-reading and in lack of knowledge of abstract words were discovered by the authors in the first test. To avoid these handicaps, a new test of names of 16 concrete objects was made. These were pronounced, and a picture of each object was shown as the object was named. When the scores which were made on the test were compared with scores of pupils in Grades 4, 6, and 8 of a New York City school, and with Grades 5A, 5B, and 6B of another school, these were the results:

Grade	Scores of Two New York City Schools	Scores of Deaf in Corresponding Grades
4	7.8	12.7
5A	8.6	....
5B	9.8	13.6
6	10.8	....
8	13.6	15.2

Gates and Chase conclude that the evidence indicates that deaf children possess, in comparison with their other linguistic abilities and in comparison with the achievements of normal children of similar reading experience, at least superior spelling ability. They conclude, too, that of the possible causes of high spelling ability—extensive reading, extensive written composition, extensive spelling drill, and effective methods of learning and teaching in spelling—the last is the one to which the difference is most probably due in this case. Working on this assumption, they analyzed the learning of new spelling words by these deaf children and found the following factors present:

A child tries to get the word by lip-reading and demonstrates his perception by pronunciation. The teacher speaks the word and demonstrates its meaning by action or object. The pupils try to pronounce the word. If they cannot get it as a whole they are assisted time after time in approximating the pronunciation of the word syllable by syllable until they can reproduce the syllables in order. Then a pupil writes on the board the word as nearly as he can, usually syllable by syllable. The teacher corrects errors by writing the word on the board and the pupils compare their own written forms with the word as the teacher has written it.

"Normal children enjoying phonic and phonetic experience

learn to depend primarily upon a phonetic rendering-translation of the sounds into letters which represent them, when attempting to recall the spelling of words. In several analytic studies, published and unpublished, of good and poor spellers, this habit was found to be almost universal." [p. 295] The authors contend that the fact that English spelling is systematically unphonetic prevents this system from functioning and that normal persons are prone to error because so many possible translations are phonetically accurate.

"The deaf, of course, are incapable of thinking first of the sounds and then recalling a combination of letters which represent them and despite the system of encouraging them to spell by recalling combinations of letters associated with the lip-movements of others or their own acts of pronunciation, it seems probable . . . that they depend mainly on another learning device. This device consists in a more careful visual study of the word forms in the final stages of learning when their written word is compared with the correct form placed on the board and in the attempt to recall not the lip-movement letter-combination associations but the visual appearance of the word during attempts to spell words not yet firmly habituated as writing habits." [p. 296]

To test attention to visual form, the list of 16 concrete words used in the last test was given to the children for one-minute study. They were asked to observe the words but were not permitted to spell them aloud or to write them. The words were then dictated. The average gain of the deaf children was 4 words, of the normal children, 2.4 words. To check on this superiority the authors gave a "Word Selection Test" which measures the speed and accuracy with which one can perceive an isolated word and immediately perceive it again in the midst of several other very similar words. This was followed by a second test, known as "Word Perception, Same-Different Test," which requires the subject to underline the pairs of words which are unlike and to leave unmarked those which are identical.

These tests are symptomatic of the kind of perceptive skill being measured here. The scores from the "Word Selection" and the "Word Perception, Same-Different Tests" are given in the following tabulation which shows the ages of average normal children which the deaf children equal in the four functions:

Deaf Group	Actual Age	Reading Age	Spelling Age	Word Selection Age	Word Perception, Same-Different
1	13.6	6.9	11.2	12.4	16.5
2	14.2	8.1	11.6	12.4	16.0
3	16.4	8.4	12.6	15.5	17.7

These investigators further report that:

There can be no doubt of the extraordinary word-perception ability of the deaf pupils. . . . The deaf owe their remarkable spelling ability primarily to a peculiarly effective type of perceiving, of reacting visually to words. . . . Normal children fail to develop this effective form of word observation because they rely mainly on the easier, perhaps more natural, yet for spelling less productive, device of phonetic translation.

Describing a method of study relating to visual perception, W. F. Book [3] reports observation and work with a case of special spelling disability. The child was in the sixth grade, was a good reader, had an IQ of 120, but had such a serious speech defect that his oral speech was not understandable. His spelling score on the sixth grade Ayres-Buckingham list at the beginning of the study was 15 per cent; at this time he had not been shown how to study spelling. His method was to spell a word as he heard it pronounced. The general plan of the method used in dealing with this case was to have the subject learn to spell by using his visual rather than his auditory imagery; special emphasis was placed upon the necessity of never spelling the word unless the visual image was present and clear. These were the steps in the process [3, pp. 386-7]:

1. Study and learn one word at a time.
2. Look carefully at it and think what it means.
3. Have it pronounced by examiner.
4. Note carefully all letters and exact order in which they come.
5. Look for syllables or unknown parts of word.
6. Observe word two or three times. Then try to see it with eyes closed. If it is not so clear that you can mentally see all its syllables and letters, open your eyes and look again. Study it carefully in this way, noticing each time you look at the word the various letters that compose it.
7. When you get so you can see the word plainly with your eyes closed, write it just as you pictured it in your mind but without pronouncing any of the letters.
8. After writing the word, compare it with your copy to make sure that the word you have written is exactly like your copy and like the picture of the word you had in mind before you began to write.

At the end of the two-weeks' period the subject had learned over 300 words; 18 days after instruction began he spelled 48 of the 50 words in the Ayres list correctly.

Visual imagery has been a subject of interest to Horn, who, in an article "Principles of Method in Teaching Spelling" in the *Eighteenth Yearbook of the National Society for the Study of Education* [24, p. 65], says:

The emphasis in presenting the word should be upon visual imagery. Not only have studies of types of imagery shown that children of the elementary school period are predominantly visual, but the direct investigation of the relative efficiency of various methods of learning to spell has quite uniformly revealed that visual presentation is an essential part of methods which give superior results. Poor spellers are relatively deficient in using visual imagery.

Horn also states his belief in the importance of recalling the visual image of the word, and suggests a method of recalling it as follows [24, p. 68]:

It is important to expend some time on drill in recalling the visual image of the word, rather than to expend all the time in impressing this image. Visual recall may be reinforced by writing the word. . . . Writing a word is an aid in learning to spell it.

Thorndike [47, p. 190], in commenting upon Horn's work, says:

The leading expert in this field, Ernest Horn, relies almost entirely on the learning of the spelling of each word by itself, having almost no confidence in generalizations of any kind in this field. We may agree with him in his skepticism concerning the value of the ordinary rules and similarities as commonly taught and still hope that a more fundamental analysis will indicate certain combinations of generalization and one by one learning as superior to the latter alone. . . . Wholesale acceptance or rejection of any procedure is risky as a method of teaching. It is often necessary to extend the analysis to each case. . . . There is evidence that much of the learning and relearning or prevention of forgetting in spelling comes as a by-product of reading. . . . A method of teaching spelling which, other things being equal, improved ability to perceive words during reading in a way beneficial to later spelling would be highly advantageous. Indeed its influence in this direction might far outweigh its influence in the day-by-day learning of the five or six hundred words assigned for study each year. In the case of any method we must consider the total effect on the learner.

A study of the mistakes which pupils make in spelling, together with an analysis of the causes of these mistakes, has been made

by Book and Harter, who reported their findings in the *Journal
of Educational Research* for February 1929 [4]. Data for their
work came from the schools of Bloomington, Illinois, and included results from 3,096 test papers from the grades (520 per
grade), 608 compositions from high school students, and 1,492
themes from college freshmen. Mistakes analyzed totaled 18,840.
Errors were grouped according to the grade in which they oc-
curred, all the misspellings for each word being assembled to determine, if possible, the cause of the mistakes, the relative
frequency per grade, and the stage of learning which caused
greatest difficulty.

The investigators made a careful distinction between errors and
mistakes. Study revealed that all mistakes could be grouped under 18 types of errors, and that these were the real causes of all
spelling mistakes and were synonymous with the psychological
factors which produced them. Among the main errors, the following, listed under the two chief causes of errors in spelling,
were found [4, pp. 106-118] :

  1. Errors caused by inadequate mental control:
         20% errors—omission of letters.
          7% transposition of letters.
     about 5% repetition or adding letter.

  2. Errors caused by phonetic spelling—ignorance of word:
         26% spelling by sound.
          7% (freshman themes) mispronunciation of word.
          2% homonyms.
          5% hearing and perceiving word incorrectly.
          7% ignorance of word.

Book and Harter feel that to prevent mistakes due to phonetic
spelling and ignorance of the word, pupils must be taught to
observe words carefully, to test for accuracy, and never to guess
at the spelling of any unfamiliar word. According to these
investigators, not only should the correct pronunciation be given
but a visual analysis of the word should be made and both meaning and visual form stressed.

Another study of causes of errors was made by Davis [8, p.
620], who analyzed and classified the spelling difficulties of 275
children from Grades 3B to 6B. Out of 501 listed difficulties
encountered in spelling by the 275 children, 415 were accounted
for and the frequency of each difficulty listed as follows:

DIFFICULTIES ENCOUNTERED IN SPELLING BY THE 275 PUPILS AND THE
FREQUENCY OF EACH DIFFICULTY

DIFFICULTY　　　　　　　　　　　　　　　　　　　　　　　　　　　FREQUENCY
1. Has not mastered the steps in learning to spell a word........ 88
2. Writes poorly 88
3. Cannot pronounce the word being studied..................... 78
4. Has bad attitude toward spelling as shown by (*a*) failure to apply himself during the study period or by (*b*) seeming lack of interest 71
5. Does not associate the sound of the letters or the syllables with the spelling of the word..................................... 49
6. Needs more time than can be devoted to spelling in the regular class 21
7. Is discouraged because he misspelled so many words in the Monday test 20

It is possible here that other analyses than those given could have been made of these difficulties. Better visual perception is not included by the author as a primary need, though the failure of auditory perception as a means of learning given in number 5 may imply the need of better visual perception.

That the relationship between sound and visual and graphic form is intimately involved in spelling is the conclusion made by Watson [50]:

Useful as it undoubtedly is, both psychologically and pedagogically, to build associations from the visual appearance of words to their reproduction by graphic movements, their phonic forms cannot be entirely disregarded. This is true for the reason that the vocal-auditory use of words is both antecedent to, and more frequent than, their visual graphic use in the development of language. For those born deaf, these considerations do not, of course, apply. This may be the explanation for deaf children's having less difficulty in spelling than do children with normal hearing.

Gates [17, p. 77] believes that inadequate visual perception of a word is the most common type of difficulty in spelling. Writers have often implied or directly stated [49, p. 34; 24, p. 65] that "visual imagery" is a predominant form of imagery among children and have used this assumption as a basis for the increased attention to visual form. Gates [17, p. 79] says:

The visual image, despite prodigious work on it, is still very much of a mystery. No one knows precisely what it is, on what mechanisms it depends, or how to measure it with accuracy. . . . In our procedure the image has been conceived as a symptom of the perceptual reaction. When the word is appropriately perceived, the image is adequate; when the habit of observation is ineffective, the image is incomplete and vague.

The same writer comments further as follows upon the "types of imagery" [16, p. 280].

> So far as we know, the primary and higher neural connections of the brain roused through one sense organ are just as modifiable and retentive as are the centers stimulated by others. Other things being equal, we learn quite as readily through one sense as another with the exception, of course, of individuals whose receiving, connecting or central mechanisms are defective. . . . Nearly all children can and do employ all of the common types of imagery. . . . The image type of the pupils is a matter that teachers may well disregard not only because it is very seldom of importance, but also because there are at present no reliable methods by which the imagery of children can be diagnosed.

The case for attention to clearer visual perception of a word would then seem to rest on the more direct relationship of this form of perception to the actual use for which the spelling of a word is ordinarily needed in life; that is, in written form. Garrison and Garrison [4, p. 357], regarding the emphasis to be placed on written spelling and the close relation between the visual presentation of the word and its spelling when written, say:

> It is almost universally agreed that emphasis should be placed on written spelling because spelling is used primarily in writing. The close relation between the visual presentation of the word and its spelling when written is apparent.

METHODS OF LEARNING WORDS AND WEEKLY PLANS

There have been reviewed in this chapter studies and expert opinions supporting points of view on these elements in method in the teaching and learning of spelling words: the test-study and the study-test plans, syllabication of words, time per week to be devoted to spelling, the number of words to be studied, teacher-directed and independent study, context and list teaching, home- and teacher-directed review, and emphasis on visual perception in the teaching of words. From the results of such studies various plans have evolved for the learning of spelling words and for the use of the school spelling time. These plans have differed just as the results of investigations and the opinions of authorities have differed. Contributing to these plans have been investigations and opinions touching other points than those reported above. Reed [43] reports an investigation by Lay showing the percentage of error per pupil resulting from certain modes of presentation of spelling words as follows [43, p. 236]:

Grades 1-6: Nonsense Syllables (About 30 children in each experiment)

Method of Presentation	Percentage of Error per Pupil
Hearing, without speech movement	3.04
Hearing, and speaking letters softly	2.69
Hearing, and speaking letters loudly	2.25
Seeing, and silent reading of letters	1.22
Seeing, and speaking letters softly	1.02
Seeing, and speaking letters loudly	0.95
Spelling aloud	1.02
Copying, and speaking letters softly	0.54

He summarizes another experiment by Baird [43, p. 236], giving results with words instead of nonsense syllables, as follows:

Method of Presentation	Percentage Misspelled
Pronounced only	6.48
Heard and spelled aloud by pupil	4.66
Only shown to pupil	2.60
Seen and spelled aloud by pupil	2.27
Seen, used, spelled, and written by pupil	1.00

Reed also reports [43, p. 231] an experiment carried on under his own supervision to discover the number of repetitions necessary to secure the maximum efficiency in learning a word. The word was written on the board, was pronounced and spelled by the teacher, and was then pronounced and spelled orally in concert by the class. This process was called one repetition. One teacher varied the number of repetitions from one to eight and taught words from those assigned for her grade. She taught one word a day for three days for each number of repetitions, giving the word before the regular class period and testing it after the period. Another teacher followed the same procedure, but varied the number of repetitions from one to five, taught five words for each number of repetitions, gave two words each day, and presented them in cycles; that is, she gave one repetition the first day, two the second day, three the third day, and so on to the fifth day. In the next five days the same procedure was repeated. The increase in number of words in the first method stopped with the fourth repetition, while the second had not reached a limit in the fifth. However, the first teacher's group started at 92.0 per cent and reached 98.6 per cent, while the second progressed from 63.5 per cent to 93.0 per cent.

There is no assurance that absolute perfection could be reached with all children by any method, and as Reed [43, p. 234] points out, the efficacy of repetition depends not only upon the number but also upon the intensity of the repetitions, the familiarity of the words, and the purpose of the learners.

Gates [16, p. 336] worked with both meaningful and meaningless materials in determining the effect of recitation upon the proportion of material recalled. He used sixteen rows of nonsense syllables and short biographies of 170 words each. The proportion of time devoted to reading without looking away from the paper and to reading with an attempt to recall varied. The result was measured by calculating the percentage of the material remembered after four hours. When all the time was devoted to reading, 15 per cent of the nonsense syllables and 16 per cent of the meaningful material were remembered. When four-fifths of the time was devoted to recitation, 48 per cent of the nonsense material and 26 per cent of the meaningful material were remembered. Throughout the experiment the greater the amount of time devoted to recitation, the greater the proportion of material recalled.

The rather general practice is to graph class or individual results of spelling study. The belief that this has value has come from such studies as the following one of Arps [2, p. 1]:

The data supporting this study were obtained by means of the Bergström Ergograph. . . . The question concerning which an experimental answer is here attempted is, whether a condition of relatively complete awareness of results is more or less favorable to efficiency than is a condition of partial awareness. To what extent, if any, does knowledge of results further efficiency; or, to what extent does a lack of knowledge curtail efficiency . . . Again, is a response, in which a knowledge of results constitutes essential features, more or less efficient than a response when such knowledge is relatively lacking?

With the limits operative for the present study both the absolute amount of work and the rate of work done under conditions of knowledge of results exceed that done under conditions of ignorance of results. . . .

Will power as conventionally regarded is inadequate to explain the efficiency differences. It is more likely that the neuro-muscular chain underlying the lifting response functions more efficiently when the afferent channels from the eye are open than when they are closed. The former condition appears provocative of greater functional changes in the central nervous system than the latter, which changes operate to maintain attention and increase muscular efficiency.

Attention may well be a "disinterested spectator" and a mere sign for the degree of central functional changes which become determinants of the efficiencies of the various work periods. . . . [2, p. 40]

Gates [17, pp. 16, 31, 32] reports as follows the correlation between ability to spell and recognition of spelling of word, ability to discriminate small differences, and intelligence:

With recognition of spelling of a word............................ .63
With ability to discriminate small differences between pairs of words .55
With intelligence .... .42

This seems to indicate that visual perception when used as a factor in the learning of words is as much to be relied upon as basic intelligence.

Tidyman [49, p. 34], commenting on visual presentation, says:

The first step is to get a clear, accurate mental picture of the whole word in visual, auditory and speech motor form.

And again [49, p. 37]:

Since visual learners are in the majority visual presentation should be the basic method. . . . Variety of presentation is equally important.

Taking the ground that the learning of spelling depends upon the adequacy of specific bonds and hierarchies of bonds, LaRue [32, pp. 181,183] lists the bonds which must be formed as these:

So it comes about that we can think of a word in four ways: how it looks, how it sounds, how we speak it, and how we write it—or we may combine these ways.

From the beginning of experience, then, to the last letter in the spelling of a word, the following connections are necessary:
1. Bonds for the object (action, or what not).
2. Bonds between object and word, and between word and object.
3. Bonds for word as a whole, heard, seen, and spoken.
4. Bonds for letters of the alphabet, seen, named, and written.
5. Bonds between each letter and its sound, or sounds.
6. Bonds-in-series for letters-in-order, especially written.

Schmidt [44, p. 111] summarizes the matter of word learning in this way:

Four types of associations in spelling:
a. The spelling of some people is governed by the appearance of the word as a whole. They depend upon the visual image.
b. When there is much oral spelling, the learner forms associations between the letters of the word as they are heard when uttered either by himself or by others. The resulting auditory image in such cases may render considerable assistance in spelling.
c. If a person spells a word orally a great many times, connections are

also formed between the movements of the vocal organs in uttering the letters, so that when he starts to spell the word the vocal organs tend to finish the process automatically.

d. Sometimes spelling is controlled by the feeling of movement required to write. Familiar words, like names which we have written in a definite way for a long time, cannot be written in a new form without special effort. Evidently the movements of the hand have been automatized; that is, their succession has become habituated.

Reed [43, p. 247] lists these points as a guiding basis for a spelling method:

1. Get the presentation of the words through as many sensory modes as possible. See them, hear them, pronounce them, and write them.
2. Give special attention to the difficult letters in a word.
3. Study the words singly or in columns rather than in sentences.
4. Present long words in syllables.
5. Study homonyms separately.
6. Study words similar in spelling in groups.
7. Give special attention to the order of the letters.
8. Use oral study rather than silent study.
9. Use any of these with repetition until the habit is perfected.

Gates [17, p. 78] suggests the following as a plan of work for the week and as a method of study:

1. Take 20-30 consecutive words from the list for a test (The teacher keeps an individual record for each child of his progress on this list.)
2. Words missed by each pupil should form his spelling project for week. He should write each word on a card and study it later until learned. Keep unlearned words in an envelope or box marked "words to learn." When mastered the card should be transferred to an envelope or box marked "words to be reviewed."
3. On Tuesday, Wednesday and Thursday each child studies his own group of words. When he has mastered his set, he should take the next 10 or so words from the list, write them on cards and study them as before.
4. On Friday, the teacher gives a review test, made up of the words most frequently misspelled on the Monday test. All words then misspelled must be relearned.

Learning to spell should become an individual project which the child undertakes largely on his own initiative. . . . He must first *be taught how to proceed.*

And again [17, p. 80]:

How to learn to spell a word:
1. Carefully pronounce the printed word by syllables or in units convenient for pronunciation. Look at each syllable very carefully during pronunciation.

2. Next, look aside or close your eyes if you like, and as you pronounce the word syllable by syllable, try to think how the word looks. If you can't remember how each syllable looks, glance at the word. Keep trying until you can "visualize" the word clearly.

3. Now write the word on paper while pronouncing it syllable by syllable. If you fail try to think how the word looks. If you cannot do that, look at the printed word again. Repeat step 2 before trying again to write it, however. When you have written the word once compare it with the printed word. If correct cover it up and write it several times, always looking at it closely and pronouncing the syllables to yourself.

4. If the word was difficult put it in the group for review and try it again the next day.

Tidyman [49, pp. 146-151] includes in his study a number of plans used by successful teachers in teaching spelling words. The following one is typical of these plans:

1. Write the word on the board and pronounce it.
   Have the children pronounce it.
2. The children give sentences with the word in it.
3. Divide the word into syllables.
4. The children pick out known words, as *or* and *corn*.
   Underline. Emphasize hard parts.
   Associate with *or* and *corn*.
5. Children spell word orally with eyes closed.
6. Children write the word two or three times.

Mossman [39, pp. 177, 179, 180] gives the following as a suggested procedure in teaching spelling:

1. The list of words which the grade is expected to learn in a term should be in the possession of the teacher. On Friday of each week she should select from the list a given number of words, picking those which are most needed in the work of the following week. The number of words for the week should be about 25.

2. Monday morning the entire class is tested on the list of the week. The children should understand that doubtful letters and erasures are to be counted wrong, as evidence of uncertainty of knowledge. The children should score their own papers and the teacher immediately check their work. This gives children immediate knowledge of what words they know and avoids longer doubt as to correct spelling. Each child should record in his own notebook the words he missed, together with the date. The teacher, from a showing of hands by the children, notes the number missing each word. This tells her what words to teach first. Children should understand that the words are those needed for the week. This test should be written.

3. The day's list of words should include the day's portion of new words

plus enough review words to bring the total number to ten. The number taught each study day should be the same.

4. The method of teaching a list of words is:

a) The teacher writes the word on the board, at the same time pronouncing it distinctly, so that syllables are heard.

b) The children look at the word, pronouncing it distinctly, together and individually.

c) The children and the teacher note the difficult part of the word, mentioning the difficulty in a *positive* way.

d) The children practice visualizing the word until they can visualize every letter clearly when the eyes are shut. Varied method, to hold interest, is here desirable.

e) The children try writing the word from visual imagery and checking with the copy on the blackboard. If wrong, more practice in visualizing is necessary. If right, the word should be again written and checked. If the child can write the word three times correctly, it is temporarily mastered.

f) Similarly each new word is taught.

g) Similarly each review word is taught but less time should be given to the teaching of each review word.

h) The entire list previously written and covered should be exposed for a *brief* review period in which each child is taught to work on the word most troublesome to him. If this review period is longer than a minute or so it may lead to laxity.

Test the ten words just taught.

i) Each child scores his own words and enters errors with the date in his notebook. He enters his total score in the notebook he is keeping as a record of his progress.

On the page arranged for keeping scores on the ten-word tests of teaching days, the child enters his score for the test, together with the date on which the test is taken. It will be noted that there are in his notebook two record sheets for scores, one for 25-word tests and one for 10-word tests. By keeping these on separate pages the results of learning are comparable, and the results of testing to find out ability are comparable.

5. Friday the entire class is tested upon all the words of the week.

Saying the letters has not been included as a learning method. Spelling is a written function, not an oral one. As soon as children master the *method* of studying spelling, they may be given the list of a month and left to learn at will, subject to stated tests. This could reasonably happen with a sixth or seventh grade.

The methods of work used in the present study were compiled from these accepted plans for teaching spelling and were changed as the effect of various factors became obvious, as is shown in Chapter IV.

CHAPTER III

THE SETTING FOR THE STUDY

Data for the testing of the various factors in this experimental
spelling study were collected from the Fox Meadow School of
Scarsdale, New York, during the school years of 1928-1929 and
1929-1930. During the period of 1928-1929 the data came from
seven classes, which included one high and one low section of
Grades 3, 4, 5, and 6. In the latter part of the year the low third
grade section became a high third, and the low sixth grade became
a high sixth grade. For these two grades the data from only one
section are included, while each other grade is represented by two
sections. A seventh grade was added to the classes taught the
second year of the study, thus making ten groups from which
results are included in the data.

Fox Meadow School is a public school in a new residential
district of Scarsdale. The building is modern and well equipped
and the work carried on there provides for a fairly free activity
program. The teachers are progressive in attitude and are well
trained. As is shown in Table I in the Appendix, page 85, eight
of the twelve teachers conducting the experiment held degrees,
while the other four were working toward degrees. Every teacher
included in the experiment is a part-time student taking work
either at Teachers College, Columbia University, or at New York
University.

Table II in the Appendix, page 86, shows the standing of the
various grades at the beginning of the first year of study on the
basis of the National Intelligence Test, the Woody-McCall Arithmetic Test, the Thorndike-McCall Reading Test, and the Morrison-
McCall Spelling Test, while Table III in the Appendix, page 86,
gives similar data on the grades included at the middle of the second year of the study. These test standings indicate that there
had been consistent drill teaching in the skill subjects both before
and during the time the study was in progress. A controlled study
such as the present one did not, then, subject the children to a dif-

ferent drill situation from that to which they had been accustomed.

Appropriate grade lists from Pearson and Suzzallo, *Essentials of Spelling* [42] were used throughout the two years' experiment. This study is not in any sense one dealing with the choice of or the rating of spelling lists for grade use. Rather, the essential point emphasized in the experiment was that the lists used in any grade should be of the same degree of difficulty as the lists presented to the children in each of the other grades. The lists in *Essentials of Spelling* are rather well graded in difficulty, as is shown by the fact that the mean number wrong in the initial tests was easily equalized. The initial word lists for each class were taken from the appropriate grade lists.

The study was divided into eight five-weeks' periods; four in the first year and four in the second. Each week contained five spelling periods of 15 minutes each. An initial test was given at the beginning of each five-weeks' period, covering the next 80 words in the spelling list. This test was a regular procedure in each of the grades in question. Results showed 28 as the nearest mean number of words incorrect throughout the groups. A few times during the study, when these grade lists proved to be too easy or too difficult for the grade, other unstudied portions of the grade lists were selected until the list in question was equalized with the others. The equalization of the groups was thus essentially one of equalization of the learning load.

A final dictation test covering the 80 words was given at the end of the five-weeks' teaching period. These results were then a combination of immediate- and delayed-recall. They include immediate-recall for the words studied in the fifth week; a one-week's delayed-recall for the words taught in the fourth week; a two-weeks' delayed-recall for those taught in the third week; a three-weeks' delayed-recall for those taught in the second week; and a four-weeks' delayed recall for the words that were taught in the first week.

Whenever the experimental factor was not used in all the grades, both younger and older children were included in the study of the factor. This is true in the case of the use of words in lists, as compared with their use in sentences. It is also true in the case of individual study as compared with class-directed study. When there was a possibility of practice effect, the factors were rotated in the various classes, in the following manner:

Without Review		With Home Review
3B EF_1 — EF_3	....	EF_1 — EF_3
3A EF_3 — EF_1	....	EF_3 — EF_1

The experimental factors in this example are:

> EF_1 — words used in lists only with teacher-directed study.
> EF_3—words in lists only with individual study.

Each application of a factor covered a controlled study of five weeks, including five fifteen-minute periods a week.

A uniform method of word study was used during that part of the investigation dealing with the comparison of teacher-directed and individual work, as well as during the study of words from lists only as compared with their use in a list-context method. This method includes elements recommended by Horn [24, p. 72], Tidyman [49, p. 71], and Mossman [39, p. 179].

In the teacher-directed study, the teacher used the directions given in taking up each individual word. For the classes using individual study, the steps were printed on a large piece of oak tag and posted in the front of each room. In the case of individual study, the actual experimentation was preceded by a week's directed study, so that the method might be familiar to all the children. The rotation of the use of individual or teacher-directed study eliminated the effect of unfamiliarity with the method, if such unfamiliarity did exist.

With the exception of the method using "other factors in form" [Introduction, p. 3], in which the child compares his written word with the preceding one in his own writing and identifies it among similar words, the directions for the studying of words used throughout the experimentation were as follows:

1. Look at the word. Say it looking at it closely as you pronounce it distinctly.
2. Close your eyes and recall the word syllable by syllable as you whisper it. Say the letters by syllables.
3. Look at the book (or word on the board) to see if you said the letters correctly. If not, repeat steps 1 and 2.
4. Write the word and check to see if you are right. If not, repeat steps 1 through 4.
5. Write it again and look to see if you are correct. If you have written the word three times correctly, assume that you have learned it for the day. If you make a single mistake begin with step 1 and repeat the study.

CHAPTER IV

THE REPORT OF THE PRESENT STUDY

The methods of work used in the present study were compiled from the accepted plans for teaching spelling referred to in Chapter II and were changed as the effect of various factors became obvious, as is shown later in the present chapter.

The study of words entirely in isolation as compared with isolated study combined with the writing of the words in sentences, individual and teacher-directed study, and additional home study were the factors analyzed during the first year.

Individual and Teacher-Directed Study with the List Method and the List-Context Method

In teacher-directed study—the taking up of each new word in turn by the teacher—the children worked together, spending a uniform amount of time on each word missed by any individual in the class. The word was written on the board as a whole and in syllables in the presence of the class. The children worked at the same time but not in unison; that is, each child said the word and spelled it softly and at his own rate of speed. The children who did not miss any words in the preliminary test of the words for the week were excused from study. The words to be studied included all those missed in the sixteen-word list for the week.

In the individual-study plan the child studied the words which he himself missed on the preliminary Monday test. The same study-method was carried out as that used by the teacher-directed groups, with the exception of a controlled division of time on the various words.

In the factor "study of words from lists" the children studied on Tuesday the words they missed on the Monday test. Another test was given on Wednesday; on Thursday they studied again words missed on Wednesday; and on Friday another test was given, followed by further study on the words missed. This testing was list testing, the words being studied entirely apart from context.

In the factor called "list-context method" the preliminary testing and the Tuesday studying were carried on in the same way. On Wednesday, instead of another test, each child wrote the words missed in his own sentences. In the case of individual study, he wrote the words he himself had missed; in the case of teacher-directed study, he wrote the total list missed by the class. On Thursday in the list-context method, the teacher dictated all words for the week in sentences to be written by the children. The entire list was again dictated as a list on Friday, and the words missed were restudied. As will be noted, the words were studied in isolation on one day and written in sentences on two other days. All the words missed on any day were studied in isolation under the teacher's direction.

These were the directions followed by teachers in each of the different methods:

1. *Use of Words in Lists Only with Teacher-Directed Study.*

Monday:

Open the book and pronounce all the words for the week. Use each word in a sentence or have the children use the words in sentences. Dictate the list for the week. Write the correct form of each word on the board or let children use their books and correct the words missed. The children with 100 per cent are excused from study for the week.

Tuesday:

The teacher teaches the words according to the study method outlined above.

Wednesday:

Repeat the Monday's test. Again let children correct the words from the teacher's writing them on the board or from their texts.

Thursday:

The teacher makes a list of all words missed on the Wednesday's test and reteaches them as on Tuesday.

Friday:

Give a test on all words for the week. Let the children correct them as before. The teacher again reteaches all words missed.

Keep a class graph showing progress on each week's work on the class bulletin board.

2. *Use of Words in Lists Only with Individual Study.*

Monday:

Open the book and pronounce all the words for the week. Use each word in a sentence or have the children use the words in sentences. Dictate the list for the week. Write the correct form of each word on the board or let the children use their books and correct the words missed. The children with 100 per cent are excused from study for the week.

Tuesday:

Each child studies the words he missed according to the study method outlined above.

Wednesday:

Repeat the Monday's test. Again let children correct the words from the teacher's writing them on the board or from their texts.

Thursday:

Each child makes a list of all the words missed on the Wednesday's test and restudies them as on Tuesday.

Friday:

Give a test on all the words for the week. Let the children correct them as before. Each child again restudies all the words missed.

Keep a class graph showing progress on each week's work on the class bulletin board.

3. *Use of List-Context Method with Teacher-Directed Study.*

Monday:

Open the book and pronounce all the words for the week. Use each word in a sentence or have the children use the words in sentences. Dictate the list for the week. Write the correct form of each word on the board or let the children use their books and correct the words missed. The children with 100 per cent are excused from study for the week.

Tuesday:

The teacher teaches the words according to the study method outlined above.

Wednesday:

The children write the class list of words missed for the week in their own sentences. They may use more than one word in a sentence if they care to. The children correct these from the teacher's writing them on the board and the teacher teaches the words missed.

Thursday:

The teacher dictates the words in the week's list in sentences. The children correct these from the board and the teacher reteaches any missed.

Friday:

Give a list test on all the words for the week. Correct the papers and reteach all words missed.

Keep on the class bulletin board a class graph showing progress on each week's work.

4. *Use of List-Context Method with Individual Study.*

Monday:

Open the book and pronounce all the words for the week. Use each word in a sentence or have the children use the words in sentences. Dictate the list for the week. Write the correct form of each word on the board or let children use their books and correct the words missed. The children with 100 per cent are excused from study for the week.

Tuesday:

Each child studies the words he missed according to the study method outlined above.

Wednesday:

Each child writes the words he missed in his own sentences. He then corrects these from his text or from a written list on the board, and restudies the ones missed.

Thursday:

The teacher dictates sentences with all the words for the week in them. These are corrected and each child restudies the words he missed.

Friday:

Give a test on all the words for the week. Let the children correct them as before. Each child studies any words he missed.

Keep on the class bulletin board a class graph showing progress on each week's work.

The two factors—study of words from lists only, and the inclusion of the writing of the words in sentences as an element in method—were first analyzed and then compared. As is shown by the detailed description of the preceding method, the use of words in oral sentences was the same in both instances. Individual words were also studied in isolation from context in each case. In the list-context method, however, the words were written in sentences on two days of study, while in the list method this time was given to testing and to additional study of words out of context.

The other factors, in addition to these two in method, were concerned with the directing of study. Class study, as described above, was the method in which the teacher directed the study;

in individual study the child was directed by the teacher in learning the word but worked alone on his individual list of words.

These four factors were combined in the following manner: three classes studied words from lists, with teacher-directed study for five weeks, after which they studied another group of 80 words for five weeks, also from lists, but using individual study; four other classes studied the first lists of 80 words, using the words in sentences with teacher-directed study, followed by five weeks of study with another eighty-word list, using the words in sentences with individual study. These factors were then rotated; one class used lists and teacher-directed study first, following this method with lists and individual study. Another class reversed the order of application of the experimental factors.

As each class was using a different eighty-word list in each period of five weeks, the words being chosen in sequence from the correct grade list of the Pearson-Suzzallo spellers, the equating of the learning load was done by equalizing the number of words incorrect on the initial tests. The order of the application of these four factors is given in Table I, page 50.

Table II, page 50, gives the results obtained with the groups using first lists with directed study for five weeks and then lists with individual study for a five-weeks' period. In Table II and in following tables in which data on initial tests are given, the number under the "Initial Test" column is the mean number of words wrong—28 in each case; while under the "Final Test" column the mean given is the gain in words. The higher this mean gain is, therefore, the better the results from the method used. In every case the means are given, first, correct to the first decimal, then, correct to the nearest whole number. Correctness to the nearest whole number is taken as a basis for further computation.

The difference between the scores on the initial and on the final test is found for each individual child, while the mean gain is computed from these individual changes.

In Table II the factor present throughout is the use of lists, while the method of study, directed or individual, is present in equal amounts.

Table III, page 51, gives results from classes using the list-context method with directed study, combined with results from classes using the list-context method with individual study. Here

TABLE I

ORDER OF EXPERIMENTAL FACTORS

GRADE	FACTOR IN FIRST FIVE WEEKS	FACTOR IN SECOND FIVE WEEKS
3B	Lists only—directed study 5 weeks	Lists only—individual study 5 weeks
3A	Lists only—individual study 5 weeks	Lists only—directed study 5 weeks
4B	List-context method—directed study 5 weeks	List-context method—individual study 5 weeks
4A	List-context method—individual study 5 weeks	List-context method—directed study 5 weeks
5B	List-context method—individual study 5 weeks	List-context method—directed study 5 weeks
5A	List-context method—directed study 5 weeks	List-context method—individual study 5 weeks
6B	Lists only—directed study 5 weeks	Lists only—individual study 5 weeks

TABLE II

RESULTS FROM THE USE OF THE LIST METHOD, WITH DIRECTED STUDY AND INDIVIDUAL STUDY EQUALLY PRESENT

$$N = 101$$

INITIAL TEST	FINAL TEST
Words Wrong	Mean Gain in Words
Mean = 27.8 = 28 σ = 14 σ_M = 1.39	Mean = 18.9 = 19 σ = 10 σ_M = .99

the use of sentences as an element in method is a constant factor throughout, while again individual and directed study are present in equal amounts.

TABLE III

RESULTS FROM THE USE OF THE LIST-CONTEXT METHOD, WITH DIRECTED STUDY AND INDIVIDUAL STUDY EQUALLY PRESENT

$N = 108$

INITIAL TEST	FINAL TEST
Words Wrong	Mean Gain in Words
Mean = 28.1 = 28 σ = 12 σ_M = 1.16	Mean = 20.6 = 21 σ = 8 σ_M = .77

A comparison may be made in these two cases between the results from the use of sentences as a factor in method, and the results from the study of words without written context. The factors of teacher-directed and individual study have been equalized, since both methods are used in an equal amount in each of the classes. The difference is a mean gain of two words in favor of the list-context method.

Table IV, page 52, shows the difference in number of words gained through use of words in lists only and through use of the list-context method. In Table IV and the following tables giving the difference in gain from the use of two methods, the sigma of the difference and the experimental coefficient (EC) are both included. If explanation is desired concerning the use of the sigma of the difference, see Garrett [13, pp. 128-134]. It is well to bear in mind that the sigma of the difference should be at least three times the difference to insure practical certainty that the true difference will be greater than zero. The technique of computing the experimental coefficient is not so well known. McCall [35, pp. 154-158] devised it to interpret the standard deviation of the difference. To quote:

The formula for its computation is so constructed that an experimental coefficient of 1.0 means that we can be *practically certain* that the true D is somewhere above zero. An EC of 0.5 means that we can be only half certain that the true D is above zero. An EC of 2.0 means we can be doubly certain that the true D is above zero. . . . For the true D to be zero, would be to make the two EF's of equal effectiveness. For it to become —1.0, would be to reverse the conclusion indicated by the obtained D. So whenever the EC is less than 1.0, the experimenter should state that one of his EF's is *probably* more effective than the other. The less the EC becomes, the more wary the experimenter should be. This does not mean that the experimenter is justified in advising practical action on the basis of his experiment only when the EC is 1.0 or above. So long as the EC is above zero, the true D more probably lies in the direction of the obtained D than, in the opposite direction.

TABLE IV

COMPARISON OF THE GAIN IN WORDS THROUGH A LIST METHOD, AND A LIST-CONTEXT METHOD, WITH THE USE OF TEACHER-DIRECTED AND INDIVIDUAL STUDY EQUALLY PRESENT

$N = 101$	$N = 108$
LISTS	SENTENCES
Mean Gain in Words	Mean Gain in Words
Mean = 18.9 = 19 σ = 10 σ_M = .99	Mean = 20.6 = 21 σ = 8 σ_M = .77

The difference is two words in favor of the list-context method difference = 1.25
EC in favor of the use of the list-context method = .57

Since factors of directed study and individual study were equally present in these results, the difference found would seem

TABLE V

RESULTS FROM DIRECTED STUDY, WITH THE USE OF THE LIST METHOD AND THE LIST-CONTEXT METHOD EQUALLY PRESENT

$N = 108$

INITIAL TEST	FINAL TEST
Words Wrong	Mean Gain in Words
Mean = 28.2 = 28 σ = 13 σ_M = 1.26	Mean = 20.7 = 21 σ = 9 σ_M = .87

to be due to the presence or absence of written sentences in the method of study. By combining results from the groups using lists with directed study and those using the list-context method with directed study and comparing these results with the results from the groups using individual study throughout, and having the factors of the list method and the list-context method equally present, it is possible to see the influence of individual and directed work. Tables V, VI, and VII show this influence.

In these results, each of the factors giving more favorable

TABLE VI

RESULTS FROM INDIVIDUAL STUDY, WITH THE USE OF THE LIST METHOD AND THE LIST-CONTEXT METHOD EQUALLY PRESENT

$N = 102$

INITIAL TEST	FINAL TEST
Words Wrong	Mean Gain in Words
Mean = 27.6 = 28	Mean = 18.8 = 19
$\sigma = 12$	$\sigma = 9$
$\sigma_M = 1.19$	$\sigma_M = .89$

TABLE VII

DIFFERENCE IN NUMBER OF WORDS GAINED THROUGH THE USE OF DIRECTED AND OF INDIVIDUAL STUDY, WITH THE USE OF THE LIST AND THE LIST-CONTEXT METHOD EQUALLY PRESENT

$N = 108$	$N = 102$
DIRECTED STUDY	INDIVIDUAL STUDY
Mean Gain in Words	Mean Gain in Words
Mean = 20.7 = 21	Mean = 18.8 = 19
$\sigma = 9$	$\sigma = 9$
$\sigma_M = .87$	$\sigma_M = .89$

Difference in favor of directed study = 2 words

σ difference = 1.24

EC in favor of directed study as compared with individual study = .6

results—directed study and use of the list-context method—has combined with it in each case the effect of one or the other of the less favorable factors—the use of words in lists only and individual study.

Table VIII shows the effect on learning when the two more favorable factors, list-context method and directed study, are combined; Table IX shows the results from the combination of the two less favorable elements, use in lists and individual study.

TABLE VIII

RESULTS FROM THE USE OF WORDS IN THE LIST-CONTEXT METHOD, WITH DIRECTED STUDY

$N = 57$

INITIAL TEST	FINAL TEST
Words Wrong	Gain in Words
Mean = 28.4 = 28 σ = 13 σ_M = 1.72	Mean = 21.9 = 22 σ = 9 σ_M = 1.19

TABLE IX

RESULTS FROM THE USE OF WORDS IN LISTS ONLY, WITH INDIVIDUAL STUDY

$N = 50$

INITIAL TEST	FINAL TEST
Words Wrong	Gain in Words
Mean = 27.7 = 28 σ = 12 σ_M = 1.69	Mean = 17.6 = 18 σ = 10 σ_M = 1.41

Table X shows the significance of difference of the two methods.

In the fall of 1929 the method which had given the best results, teacher-directed study with the use of sentences as a part of the method of learning, the list-context method, was repeated with all classes from low third grade through low

TABLE X

SIGNIFICANCE OF THE DIFFERENCE BETWEEN THE LIST-CONTEXT METHOD WITH DIRECTED STUDY, AND USE OF WORDS IN LISTS WITH INDIVIDUAL STUDY

$N = 57$	$N = 50$
List-Context Method—Directed Study	*Lists Only—Individual Study*
Gain in Words	Gain in Words
Mean = 21.9 = 22	Mean = 17.6 = 18
σ = 9	σ = 10
σ_M = 1.19	σ_M = 1.41

Difference in favor of the list-context method with teacher-directed study = 4 words

σ difference = 1.84

EC in favor of the list-context method with teacher-directed study = .78

seventh grade. This gave 108 additional cases, again with a mean gain of 22 words. Combining this group with the first group of 57 cases gave the results shown in Table XI.

TABLE XI

RESULTS FROM THE USE OF TEACHER-DIRECTED STUDY, LIST-CONTEXT METHOD

$N = 165$

INITIAL TEST	FINAL TEST
Words Wrong	Gain in Words
Mean = 28.4 = 28	Mean = 22.1 = 22
σ = 14	σ = 10
σ_M = 1.09	σ_M = .78

The difference in the mean gain between teacher-directed study, using the list-context method, and the method of using words in lists only, with individual study, is again 4 words, with an increased experimental coefficient of .89. These facts are shown in Table XII, page 56.

TABLE XII

GAINS UNDER LIST-CONTEXT METHOD, TEACHER-DIRECTED STUDY, AND LISTS ONLY, INDIVIDUAL STUDY

$N = 165$	$N = 50$
List-Context Method—Directed Study	*Lists, Individual Study*
Gain in Words	Gain in Words
Mean = 22.1 = 22 σ = 10 σ_M = .78	Mean = 17.6 = 18 σ = 10 σ_M = 1.41

Difference = 4
σ difference = 1.61

EC in favor of the list-context method with teacher-directed study = .89

INDIVIDUAL AND DIRECTED STUDY WITH THE USE OF LIST METHOD AND THE LIST-CONTEXT METHOD, WITH HOME-WORK REVIEW AS AN ADDED FACTOR

During the second ten weeks each class followed exactly the same procedure that it had followed during the first ten weeks.

TABLE XIII

RESULTS FROM ALL GROUPS WITH HOME STUDY AND ALL GROUPS WITHOUT HOME STUDY

$N = 210$		$N = 186$	
All Groups, No Home Study		*All Groups, with Home Study*	
INITIAL TEST	FINAL TEST	INITIAL TEST	FINAL TEST
Words Wrong	Gain in Words	Words Wrong	Gain in Words
Mean = 27.9 = 28 σ = 14 σ_M = .98	Mean = 19.75 = 20 σ = 9 σ_M = .62	Mean = 28.1 = 28 σ = 12 σ_M = .88	Mean = 21.45 = 21 σ = 11 σ_M = .81

The difference here in favor of review = 1 word
σ difference = 1.02
EC in favor of review = .35

The same two methods were repeated and given in the same order, with the one addition of home-work review. On Tuesday and Thursday nights of each week the words of the week were given for home work, to be studied with the study method that was used in the classroom. In the case of directed study this meant the total list missed by the class for the week; in the case of individual study, the child's own list. This resulted in

TABLE XIV

COMPARISON OF WORDS GAINED BY SCHOOL STUDY, AND WORDS GAINED BY SCHOOL STUDY PLUS HOME STUDY

Method: Words in Lists Only, Teacher-Directed Study

$N = 51$ $N = 48$

SCHOOL STUDY ONLY		SCHOOL STUDY PLUS HOME STUDY	
INITIAL TEST	FINAL TEST	INITIAL TEST	FINAL TEST
Words Wrong	Gain in Words	Words Wrong	Gain in Words
Mean $= 27.8 = 28$	Mean $= 19.4 = 19$	Mean $= 27.6 = 28$	Mean $= 21.2 = 21$
$\sigma = 14$	$\sigma = 9$	$\sigma = 12$	$\sigma = 10$
$\sigma_M = 1.96$	$\sigma_M = 1.26$	$\sigma_M = 1.73$	$\sigma_M = 1.41$

TABLE XV

COMPARISON OF WORDS GAINED BY SCHOOL STUDY, AND BY SCHOOL STUDY PLUS HOME STUDY

Method: Teacher-Directed Study, List-Context Method

$N = 57$ $N = 47$

SCHOOL STUDY ONLY		SCHOOL STUDY PLUS HOME STUDY	
INITIAL TEST	FINAL TEST	INITIAL TEST	FINAL TEST
Words Wrong	Gain in Words	Words Wrong	Gain in Words
Mean $= 28.4 = 28$	Mean $= 21.9 = 22$	Mean $= 28.4 = 28$	Mean $= 20.7 = 21$
$\sigma = 13$	$\sigma = 9$	$\sigma = 14$	$\sigma = 12$
$\sigma_M = 1.72$	$\sigma_M = 1.19$	$\sigma_M = 2.04$	$\sigma_M = 1.73$

additional time on the week's words of about a half-hour. Table XIII gives the results from all groups with home study and all groups without home study.

The additional time given to home-work study of the words helped the classes in which the less efficient methods had been used, but did not give additional gain for the classes using the teacher-directed, list-context method. This is shown in Tables XIV, XV, XVI, and XVII.

TABLE XVI

COMPARISON OF WORDS GAINED BY SCHOOL STUDY, AND BY SCHOOL STUDY PLUS HOME STUDY

Method: Words in Lists Only, Individual Study

$N = 50$ $\qquad\qquad\qquad\qquad$ $N = 49$

SCHOOL STUDY ONLY		SCHOOL STUDY PLUS HOME STUDY	
INITIAL TEST	FINAL TEST	INITIAL TEST	FINAL TEST
Words Wrong	Gain in Words	Words Wrong	Gain in Words
Mean = 27.7 = 28	Mean = 17.6 = 18	Mean = 28.3 = 28	Mean = 21.4 = 21
σ = 12	σ = 10	σ = 15	σ = 11
σ_M = 1.69	σ_M = 1.41	σ_M = 2.14	σ_M = 1.57

TABLE XVII

COMPARISON OF WORDS GAINED BY SCHOOL STUDY AND BY SCHOOL STUDY PLUS HOME STUDY

Method; List-Context, Individual Study

$N = 52$ $\qquad\qquad\qquad\qquad$ $N = 42$

SCHOOL STUDY ONLY		SCHOOL STUDY PLUS HOME STUDY	
INITIAL TEST	FINAL TEST	INITIAL TEST	FINAL TEST
Words Wrong	Gain in Words	Words Wrong	Gain in Words
Mean = 27.6 = 28	Mean = 19.0	Mean = 28.2 = 28	Mean = 22.5 = 22
σ = 11	σ = 8	σ = 13	σ = 10
σ_M = 1.52	σ_M = 1.12	σ_M = 2.01	σ_M = 1.54

Table XVIII gives the experimental coefficients for the results from home study compared with the results from no home study under the different methods.

TABLE XVIII

EXPERIMENTAL COEFFICIENTS OF HOME STUDY COMPARED WITH NO HOME STUDY, UNDER THE DIFFERENT METHODS

Lists only, directed study

> M gain no review = 19 words.
> M gain with review = 21 words.
> Difference in favor of review = 2 words.
> σ difference = 1.89.
> EC in favor of review = .38.

List-context method, directed study

> M gain no review = 22 words.
> M gain with review = 21 words.
> Difference in favor of no review = 1 word.
> σ difference = 1.85.
> EC in favor of no review = .19.

Lists only, individual study

> M gain no review = 18 words.
> M gain with review = 21 words.
> Difference in favor of review = 3 words.
> σ difference = 2.11.
> EC in favor of review = .51.

List-context method, individual study

> M gain no review = 19 words.
> M gain with review = 22 words.
> Difference in favor of review = 3 words.
> σ difference = 1.90.
> EC in favor of review = .57.

All groups home study vs. all groups no home study

> M gain no review = 20 words.
> M gain with review = 21 words.
> Difference in favor of review = 1 word.
> σ difference = 1.02.
> EC in favor of review = .35.

TEACHER-DIRECTED STUDY WITH THE USE OF LIST-CONTEXT METHOD, WITH CONCENTRATION ON THE VISUAL FORM OF THE WORD AS AN ADDED FACTOR

Definite changes in method, in which attention was concentrated on the visual form of the word, were made during the period of

1929-1930. The method of work which had given the best results, that is, teacher-directed study with the use of the list-context method, was continued. The change made over the former method of study was to present the words in visual form, with a lantern slide, instead of writing them on the blackboard. The only exception to presentation with the lantern was made on Wednesdays, when the children used the words in their own sentences. In this case the list of words was written on the board as it had been throughout the previous part of the study. With this change of word-presentation method, the plan for the week now was:

Monday:

Present each word in turn with the lantern slide. Use the word in a sentence or have the children give sentences containing it. Dictate the list for the week. Present each word again with the lantern slide for correction. The children with 100 per cent are excused from study for the week.

Tuesday:

The teacher teaches the words according to the same study plan used throughout the experiment. Each word is presented with the lantern and exposed during the time of study. If it is a syllable word the syllable slide is also shown.

Wednesday:

The children write the class list of words for the week in their own sentences. They may use more than one word in a sentence if they care to. The list of words is on the board during the writing. The teacher presents each word with the lantern for correction. The teacher teaches the words missed, again using the slides.

Thursday:

The teacher dictates the words in the week's list in sentences. The children correct these from the slides. The teacher reteaches the words missed, again using the lantern.

Friday:

The teacher gives a test on all the words for the week. The slides are presented for correction. All words missed are retaught, using the lantern.
Keep a class graph showing progress on each week's work.

Each teacher made slides for her classes by printing the word on a plain glass slide with a stub pen and India ink. A vivid enough contrast was thus secured, so that the words could be projected on the plaster walls of the room. The shades, which were semi-transparent linen, were drawn, leaving sufficient light in the room for the children to write. When a room from which daylight had been excluded was used, the electric lights were left on.

Whenever the word being studied was made up of more than one syllable, two slides were made, one for the entire word, the other for the word divided into syllables. In all cases where the word was being *taught,* the slide with the entire word was presented first and the word pronounced. The syllable slide was then put in from the left side of the lantern, so that the first syllable of the word appeared, followed by the other syllables in order. The

TABLE XIX

ORDER OF APPLICATION OF THE METHODS USING THE LANTERN AND "OTHER FACTORS IN FORM"

GRADE	FACTOR IN FIRST FIVE WEEKS	FACTOR IN SECOND FIVE WEEKS
3B	(Still 2A class so not used in experiment)	Other form factors
3A	Lantern presentation with teacher-directed review	Lantern presentation without review
4B	Lantern presentation without review	Other form factors
4A	Lantern presentation with teacher-directed review	Lantern presentation without review
5B	Lantern presentation with teacher-directed review	Lantern presentation without review
5A	Lantern presentation without review	Other form factors
6B	Lantern presentation without review	Other form factors
6A	Lantern presentation with teacher-directed review	Other form factors
7B	Lantern presentation without review	Other form factors
7A	Lantern presentation with teacher-directed review	Lantern presentation without review

teacher in charge made a slight pause after each syllable, as the children pronounced it. Following this procedure, the entire slide was again shown and the children wrote the word three times, following the same method of study used throughout the experiment.

In order to rotate out the effect of the first use of the lantern, the elements of teacher-directed review and "other factors in form" were used in varied order with the same classes. The phrase, "other factors in form," is used for lack of a more specific term. A detailed description of the elements which it includes will be given later as well as a discussion of the use here of

TABLE XX

RESULTS FROM THE USE OF LIST-CONTEXT METHOD, TEACHER-DIRECTED STUDY, USE OF LANTERN

$N = 157$

INITIAL TEST	FINAL TEST
Words Wrong	Gain in Words
Mean = 28.3 = 28 σ = 13 σ_M = 1.00	Mean = 23.7 = 24 σ = 11 σ_M = .88

TABLE XXI

COMPARISON OF THE USE OF BLACKBOARD AND LANTERN PRESENTATION

$N = 165$	$N = 157$
USE OF BLACKBOARD	USE OF LANTERN
Mean Gain in Words	Mean Gain in Words
Mean = 22.1 = 22 σ = 10.0 σ_M = .78	Mean = 23.7 = 24 σ = 11 σ_M = .88

σ difference = 1.17

EC in favor of the use of the lantern in teaching = .62

teacher-directed review. Table XIX shows the order and the classes in which the various factors were used.

Table XX gives the results of teacher-directed study, with the list-context method and the changed factor of lantern presentation, in place of blackboard presentation.

Table XXI gives the results from the use of the list-context method, teacher-directed, with blackboard and lantern presentation of words.

DESCRIPTION AND RESULTS OF TEACHER-DIRECTED REVIEW

In the classes using teacher-directed review, the words missed by the class on Friday were retaught on Tuesday and Thursday of the following week, and were given with the words of the week in the Friday's test. The length of the spelling period was the same. Table XXII gives the results with these classes.

TABLE XXII

RESULTS FROM THE USE OF THE CONTEXT-LIST DIRECTED STUDY AND REVIEW, WORDS PRESENTED WITH A LANTERN

$N = 93$

INITIAL TEST	FINAL TEST
Words Wrong	Gain in Words
Mean = 28.4 = 28 σ = 13 σ_M = 1.35	Mean = 25.8 = 26 σ_M = 11 σ_M = 1.14

DESCRIPTION AND RESULTS OF IDENTIFYING THE WORD AMONG SIMILAR FORMS, AND OF OBSERVING THE WORD IN THE SUBJECT'S OWN WRITING

In the methods using "other factors in form" three additional factors, all of which emphasize the form of the word, are included. These were added to the best method used before, that is, teacher-directed study with the use of the lantern. It seemed improbable that any one additional factor added to the results already obtained would give measurable results, so the three factors were combined. One of these was the identification of the word in a group of similar but not identical forms, before detailed study. The word was projected by the lantern, while the teacher told the number of the sentence in which the child was to look. Below is one of the lists used for one week's work.

3B—First Week

Underline the word which is exactly like the one on the slide.

1. fix   mix   six   sift   sing   sixes
2. severe   even   sever   several   seven   seventy
3. about   oat   trout   out   stout   oust
4. stain   lane   main   rain   pain   lain
5. met   set   let   mete   get   net
6. before   far   for   love   stove   fore
7. of   lift   off   if   life   oft
8. may   say   ray   slay   aye   says
9. what   hat   that's   thatch   that'   whack
10. fish   dash   wish   dish   disk   swish
11. but   cot   cuts   cute   cat   cut
12. frown   clown   down   downy   downs   sown
13. vase   wasp   as   gas   was   asp
14. the   their   there   here   ere   where
15. tool   took   stool   wood   stood   look
16. treat   streets   meet   street   fleet   neat

The second element in "other factors in form" was the writing of the word once in syllables before writing it as a whole three times, or until correctly written three times. The third minor change was to correct the word from the slide the first time it was written as a whole, then to cover this word, and the following times to compare the words as they were written during study with the previous ones in the subject's own writing. This comparison might add to sureness in judging correctness in written form. The child in the elementary grade usually judges the form of the word in his own writing, not in print.

The organization of time during the week remained the same, but the method of study included the following additions:

(To teacher: Say at the first of each lesson: "Remember we are learning to look at the word more carefully as we study it.")

1. Look at the word on the slide.
2. Find it in the list on your paper and underline it.   (Teacher gives number of sentence.)
3. Look at the form.

4. Look at it by syllables and say them. (Teacher throws syllable slide on.)
5. Write it by syllables and correct from the slide.
6. Write it as a whole, correcting by the slide. (Teacher throws slide of whole word on.) Look at the word in your own writing.
7. Cover and write and compare with your own writing. Repeat three times.

Tables XXIII and XXIV give a comparison of results from groups using first teacher-directed study, use in sentences, presented with a lantern, for five weeks followed by five weeks with the added factors of writing words in syllables as well as in units, comparing with the subject's own writing for correction, and identifying with similar but unlike words before teaching.

The difference here in mean gains is zero; therefore, the addi-

TABLE XXIII

TEACHER-DIRECTED, LIST-CONTEXT METHOD, PRESENTED WITH LANTERN

$N = 80$

INITIAL TEST	FINAL TEST
Words Wrong	Gain in Words
Mean = 28.3 = 28 σ = 14 σ_M = 1.56	Mean = 22.9 = 23 σ = 11 σ_M = 1.23

TABLE XXIV

TEACHER-DIRECTED, LIST-CONTEXT METHOD, PRESENTED WITH LANTERN, WITH "OTHER FACTORS IN FORM" ADDED

$N = 114$

INITIAL TEST	FINAL TEST
Words Wrong	Gain in Words
Mean = 27.9 = 28 σ = 14 σ_M = 1.31	Mean = 23.4 = 23 σ = 12 σ_M = 1.12

tion of the elements stressing attention to the form of the word may be considered of no measurable value, under the conditions used here and for the length of time covered by the experiment.

Gates Reading Test VI, Visual Perception Test B_2, was given to both the classes using and those not using "other factors in form" at the beginning and end of this five-weeks' period. It seemed possible that there would be a significant difference in word perception ability as a result of the use of the element of identification of unknown words in a spelling method. Tables XXVA and B give the results of this test with the two groups. They show a difference in favor of the classes using the ele-

TABLE XXV

SCORES ON GATES READING TEST VI, VISUAL PERCEPTION TEST B_2 SELECTION OF WORDS

A. *Results from Classes Using "Other Factors in Form"*

$N = 97$

INITIAL TEST	FINAL TEST
Score Right	Score Right
Mean = 24.32 σ = 6.72 σ_M = .68	Mean = 28.92 σ = 5.40 σ_M = .55

B. *Results from Classes Not Using "Other Factors in Form"*

$N = 61$

INITIAL TEST	FINAL TEST
Score Right	Score Right
Mean = 24.28 σ = 7.04 σ_M = .90	Mean = 27.52 σ = 6.88 σ_M = .88

Difference = 1.40
σ difference = 1.03

ment of identification of the word among similar forms. The difference is not large enough to be significant in a five-weeks' period, though further experimentation might give different results over a longer time.

Description and Results of Presenting New Words for Four Days Instead of Five Days of the Week

During the last five weeks of the experiment there was a different use of the week's time. Instead of giving a Monday's test on the words for the week, the analysis of the words to be studied was made from the initial test of 80 words given to equalize the difficulty of the lists. The children who did not miss words for each week were excused as before. Throughout the experiment, the words in this eighty-word test were dictated in an oral sentence, but the children did not see them before writing them. In the previous parts of the experiment the children looked at the words before they were dictated in Monday's test for the week. By omitting the additional Monday's test, the present plan gave time on both Monday and Tuesday for the actual teaching of words.

Another change was made; namely, omitting the usual Wednesday's work of the child's writing the words in his own sentences. This had been kept a constant factor throughout the list-context, teacher-directed part of the experiment. While this method was being used, the teacher, on Thursday, dictated sentences containing the words. It seems probable that this double use of context was unnecessary. If words taught are beyond the child's vocabulary, this writing in sentences of his own composition would be an important factor in testing his acquisition of words. However, there is general agreement that a spelling lesson is not the best means of teaching vocabulary. The teacher's dictated sentences should then serve the purpose with an economy of time, since she should be more adept than a child would be in grouping the words in meaningful sentences.

Throughout the experiment, review, when it was used, extended only over a five-weeks' period. Although this study does not have as an objective the collection of data on the effect of successive reviews extended over a long period, such reviews following lengthening intervals are generally conceded to be necessary. In order not to increase the time allotment per week, these reviews must either be included as part of the regular daily periods, must be taken on a special day during the week, or must be included in the time allotment at the expense of the routine for the new words being taught. In this last five-weeks' experiment the whole of the period on Wednesday was used for review, making the plan for the week the following one:

Monday:

Teach eight of the new words, using the lantern. Dictate the words just taught and reteach the words missed.

Tuesday:

Teach the other eight new words, using the lantern. Dictate and reteach the words missed.

Wednesday:

Keep this for the review or back weeks' words—See review plan.

Thursday:

Dictate sentences with the 16 new words of the week. Correct with the lantern and reteach the words missed.

Friday:

Dictate the words of the week in a list. Correct with the lantern. Reteach the words missed.

Plan for Review

(To teacher):

1. Keep a list each week of the words missed on Friday, for later study.
2. First week—No review.
3. Second week:
    Wednesday—Dictate the words of the first week. Reteach the words missed.
4. Third week:
    Wednesday—Dictate the words of the second week. Reteach those missed.
5. Fourth week:
    Wednesday—Dictate words of third week and reteach those missed. Reteach words missed on Friday of the second week.
6. Fifth week:
    Wednesday—Dictate the words of the fourth week and reteach those missed. Review any missed on Friday of the third week.

The plan here was not primarily to test the value of any particular system of review, since an adequate one could not be worked out for as short a time as five weeks, but to discover whether four days of teaching of the words with two review repetitions would give results comparable to the five-days' plan previously used. Tables XXVI, XXVII, and XXVIII give the results of the plan.

TABLE XXVI

Teacher-Directed, List-Context Method, Lantern Presentation, 4 Days Per Week with 2 Review Repetitions

$N = 148$

Initial Test	Final Test
Words Wrong	Gain in Words
Mean $= 28.2 = 28$ $\sigma \ = 15$ $\sigma_M = \ 1.23$	Mean $= 25.9 = 26$ $\sigma \ = 14$ $\sigma_M = \ 1.15$

In this case the time for presenting and testing the new words for the week was cut one-fifth, that is, from 75 to 60 minutes. The remaining fifteen-minute period was used for review of the previous weeks' words. As will be seen from the description, this review included within a five-weeks' period an additional dictated test, with study of the words missed, and an additional study of the words missed on each regular Friday's test. Two comparisons are important here. Table XXVII gives a comparison of the use of the total 75 minutes of the week on study of the new words without review with four fifteen-minute periods for study a week on new words and fifteen minutes' review; while Table XXVIII gives the comparative results from 60 minutes' study a week with a separate fifteen-minute period for review, with 75 minutes for the new words with the words missed on Friday reviewed twice during the following week.

The two methods of review give an equal mean gain in words on the final test. Under these circumstances the distribution of time into four periods a week for the study of the new words, with one whole period for review, seems the better plan. A well planned scheme of review covering a long interval would require the lengthening of the daily periods to include the necessary scheme of daily work unless a definite time is planned for review.

TABLE XXVII

COMPARISON OF FOUR 15-MINUTE PERIODS FOR STUDY A WEEK ON NEW WORDS AND 15 MINUTES' REVIEW, WITH 75 MINUTES PER WEEK NO REVIEW

List-Context Method, Teacher-Directed, Lantern Presentation

4 periods study	*5 periods study*
1 period review	*No review*
$N = 148$	$N = 157$
FINAL TEST	FINAL TEST
Gain in Words	Gain in Words
Mean $= 25.9 = 26$	Mean $= 23.7 = 24$
$\sigma \;\; = 14$	$\sigma \;\; = 11$
$\sigma_M = 1.15$	$\sigma_M = .88$

Difference in gain in words in favor of four periods study, one period review $= 2$

$$\sigma \text{ difference} = 1.44$$
$$EC = .5$$

TABLE XXVIII

COMPARISON OF METHODS OF REVIEW

4 periods study	*5 periods study*
1 period review	*2 reviews words*
1 review all words	*missed on Friday*
1 review words missed	
Friday	
$N = 148$	$N = 93$
MEAN GAIN IN WORDS	MEAN GAIN IN WORDS
Mean $= 25.9 = 26$	Mean $= 25.8 = 26$
$\sigma \;\; = 14$	$\sigma \;\; = 11$
$\sigma_M = 1.15$	$\sigma_M = 1.14$

Difference in gain in words $= 0$

CHAPTER V

SUMMARY AND INTERPRETATION OF RESULTS

A comparison of results from the use of the following elements in the spelling method has been given in the preceding chapters: teacher-directed study as compared with individual study; study of words solely from lists as compared with isolated study combined with context study; additional home study as compared with the results of teacher-directed review; comparison of the efficiency of the blackboard and lantern slides for the presentation of words; emphasis on the form of the word before study by identification among similar forms, combined with more careful attention to the form of the word in the child's own writing; and limitation of time on new words to four fifteen-minute periods a week instead of five, with two review repetitions.

From the comparisons and studies made in the preceding chapter, the results may be summarized as follows:

1. Teacher-directed study proved more efficient than individual study.
2. The use of sentences as an element in method when combined with the use of lists gave better results than the use of lists alone.
3. Additional home study was of little value in the learning of words when the teacher-directed, list-context method was used. It helped to equalize results, however, when used with the less efficient methods.
4. The use of a lantern for the presentation of words gave better results than the use of the blackboard when a method which was the same in other respects was used.
5. The use of teacher-directed review gave better results than no review.
6. Increased emphasis on form of the word before study by identification among similar forms, when combined with the child's close observance of the word in his own writing,

as used in this experiment, did not give a measurable difference in results.

7. Four fifteen-minute periods a week for study on the new words with the remaining fifteen-minute period for systematic review gave the same gain as did five fifteen-minute periods for study when two reviews of the words missed on the Friday's test were included.

8. Each of the factors, the list-context method, teacher-directed study, lantern presentation of words, and teacher-directed review, seemed about equally significant in increasing the mean number of words gained.

9. A method which combined these favorable elements was significantly better than a method which did not include them.

The Significance of the Gains in the Number of Words Learned

The significance of the difference in the number of words gained by the use of these different elements in method may be made clearer by a conversion of the experimental coefficients into a statement of chances [35, p. 155]. This is given in Table XXIX, page 73. The first column in this table gives the factors compared in each instance; the second column indicates the one which gave better results; the third column shows the number of words gained by the more favored over the less favored factor; the fourth and fifth columns give the standard deviation of this difference in gain, and the experimental coefficients. The approximate chances given in the last column of Table XXIX are the chances that the true difference is above zero in the direction of the factor favored.

The method which gave the least gain in words was the one which combined teaching words from lists only with individual study. The one which gave the largest gain in words was the one combining the list-context method, teacher-directed study, lantern presentation, and teacher-directed review. Each of these four factors had about the same amount of importance in the final result. No one factor alone gave a convincingly significant difference in the results between it and the first method tried, but each brought a gain which makes the final resulting difference a real one when the factors are combined.

TABLE XXIX

FACTORS IN METHOD FAVORED WITH THE APPROXIMATE CHANCES THAT THE
TRUE DIFFERENCE IS ABOVE ZERO

Factors Compared	Factor Favored	Difference in Number of Words in Final Mean Gain	Sigma of Difference	Experimental Coefficient	Approximate Chances
Teacher-directed *vs.* Individual study; use of lists and sentences constant	Teacher-directed study	2	1.24	0.60	20 to 1
Lists only *vs.* List-context method; individual and directed study constant	List-context method	2	1.25	0.57	18 to 1
Thirty minutes weekly added home-work review *vs.* No home-work review; review methods mixed	Home-work review	1	1.02	0.35	5 to 1
Thirty minutes weekly added home-work review *vs.* No home-work review; list-context method, teacher-directed study constant	No home study	1	1.85	0.19	2 to 1
Teacher-directed, list-context method *vs.* Individual study, words in lists	Teacher-directed list-context method	4	1.61	0.89	155 to 1
Blackboard *vs.* Lantern presentation with list-context method; teacher-directed study constant	Use of lantern presentation	2	1.17	0.62	24 to 1
Teacher-directed review *vs.* No review with list-context method; teacher-directed study, lantern presentation constant	Teacher-directed review	2	1.44	0.50	11 to 1

TABLE XXIX (*Cont.*)

Factors Compared	Factor Favored	Difference in Number of Words in Final Mean Gain	Sigma of Difference	Experimental Coefficient	Approximate Chances
Lantern presentation context-list method; teacher-directed study *vs.* Individual study, words in lists	Lantern presentation context-list teacher-directed study	6	1.66	1.30	6,700 to 1
Lantern presentation context-list method; teacher-directed study with review *vs.* Individual study, words in lists	Lantern presentation context-list method, teacher-directed study with review	8	1.81	1.59	Highly significant
Lantern presentation context-list methods; teacher-directed study, four fifteen-minute periods per week for study with systematic review in the fifth period *vs.* The same method with five fifteen-minute periods per week for study on new words with review of repetitions included	Neither	Results same			
Five days per week on new words, no review *vs.* Four days per week on new words, one day review, with list-context method, teacher-directed study, lantern presentation constant	Four days per week with one day review	2	1.44	0.50	11 to 1

Table XXIX compares the contribution of each factor through the difference in the final gain in words, the sigma of the difference, and the approximate chances that the difference is a real one.

The Effect of the Methods on the Good, the Average, and the Poor Spellers

It is conceivable that one method in spelling might be better for the poor speller, another for the average speller, or another for the good speller. The effect on these different groups could easily be concealed in the results given only in a mean gain. In

TABLE XXX

Effect of the Use of the Different Methods with Good, Average, and Poor Spellers

	Use of Words in Lists, Individual Study	Use of Words in Context-List Method, Blackboard Presentation, Teacher-Directed Study	Use of Words in Context-List Method, Lantern Presentation, Teacher-Directed, 5 Days' Study and Review	Use of Words in Context-List Method, Lantern Presentation, Teacher-Directed, 4 Days' Study, 1 Day Review
Words Wrong in Initial Test, 40–59				
Number	9	39	27	43
Mean wrong IT ...	47	48	48	48
Mean wrong FT ...	16	12	7	6
Mean gain words ..	31	36	41	42
Per cent still unlearned of words unknown on IT	32	25	14	12½
Mean per cent accuracy on total list in FT	80	85	91	92
Words Wrong in Initial Test, 20–39				
Number	22	72	46	56
Mean wrong IT ...	28	29	29	29
Mean wrong FT ...	9	6	3	3
Mean gain words ..	19	23	26	26
Per cent still unlearned of words unknown on IT	32	21	10	10
Mean per cent accuracy on total list in FT	89	92½	96	96
Words Wrong in Initial Test, 0–19				
Number	19	46	24	49
Mean wrong IT ...	15	13	12	11
Mean wrong FT ...	5	2	0	1
Mean gain words ..	10	11	12	10
Per cent still unlearned of words unknown on IT	33	15	0	9
Mean per cent accuracy on total list in FT	95	98	100	99

order to make clearer this effect of method on good, average, and poor spellers, the cases for the various methods have been regrouped into those having between 40 and 59 words wrong out of the initial 80-word test; those having between 20 and 39 wrong; and those having between zero and 19 words wrong. Table XXX shows the mean number wrong on the initial test in the group, the mean number wrong in the final test, and the percentage wrong on the final test.

Consistent improvement in the different groups, from the standpoint of the load unlearned at the end of the final test, indicates that factors which entered into the improvement were factors basic to the learning of words in general, and not factors best used by the very good speller, or those especially suited to overcome the psychological difficulties of the very poor speller.

SUMMARY OF THE ELEMENTS IN METHOD AND THE PLAN GIVING THE MOST SATISFACTORY RESULTS

In the use of the lantern with the teacher-directed review, the results show a smaller number of words wrong in the final test with an initial mean wrong of 48 than with an initial mean wrong of 28, when the list method with individual study is used. With the present tendency to limit the number of words to be taught in the elementary school to the vocabulary need of children, it would seem unwise to consider that this gain through improvement in method should mean an increase in the learning load or in the difficulty of the words taught. It would seem better to consider that it may mean that the teaching will produce more perfect results than schools ordinarily attain at present. It also makes possible the revision of the use of the ordinary allotment of 75 minutes of time a week to allow for adequate review work.

Writing of the words in sentences as an element in method was one factor which gave significantly better results than studying or teaching from lists alone. In studies cited in Chapter II, under context and list teaching, authors [21, 25, 36] consistently agree that context spelling is less accurate than list spelling. It also seems likely that a strictly context type of teaching is not an efficient means of improving spelling in column dictation [20]. The studies which have given data on this point have used a complete context method; that is, there was no isolation of the word from surrounding meaningful material. The use of context in the present experiment may be considered more in the light of a form of test for word accuracy than of the teaching of the word. The studies referred to above have made it clear that context use of words is more difficult. It then follows that accurate use in context should mean surer mastery and in general greater accuracy in column use of words. At the same time any weakness in mastery of the word should be detected in a use of it in which the concentration of attention is removed from the word itself.

Tidyman [49, p. 39] says:

The more we become absorbed in thought and composition the less sure we are of the spelling of words. . . . We may regard a word as learned when it is used freely and with a high degree of accuracy in ordinary composition such as letter writing.

And again [p. 213]:

Our spelling has stopped short of the actual mastery of words. . . . Spelling words in content is more than spelling words in isolation. . . . In contextual use the attention is mainly given to thinking and the selection and placing of words. To be of practical value spelling must be carried to the point of free and accurate use in writing. . . . It seems wise to supplement regular drill work by the use of words in written sentences, dictation and the like.

The column test is ordinarily used for initial testing. If writing of words in columns offered the most difficult situation for the use of words, it could be taken as a more dependable diagnosis of the child's ability and hence as an adequate form of initial testing. Guiler [20] found, however, "oral recall," the pronunciation of a word with its use in a meaningful sentence, followed by its writing on the part of the child, a less efficient means of detecting errors than the use of written recall, in which the child sees the word in its most usually misspelled form, and writes it correctly.

Horn [24, pp. 60, 63] says:

The teacher must expect erratic spelling; she must not expect a single correct spelling or a single misspelling to be a sufficient measure of the ability of a child.

And again:

Accordingly, better provision should be made to insure that each child work on his own special difficulties and on no others.

Since it seems probable that a column form of initial test is not the most adequate measure of the true ability of a child, it is a little difficult to be sure that one's "special difficulties" have been discovered by this one kind of test. Looking at the matter in this light, the use of words in sentences is an additional test of accuracy of acquisition of words because they are used in a situation which presents more difficulty than does column testing.

It seems probable that some of the reasons for the efficacy of teacher-directed study and the use of the lantern as a means of presenting words are the same.

Tidyman [49, pp. 37-38] says:

. . . Equally important is the active direction of the beginning drill work by the teacher. Only thus may the teacher be sure of the active attention of the children. . . . In order to be effective, this first drill work must be accompanied by a high degree of attention.

Watson [50, p. 368], in speaking of necessary spelling habits, says:

Correct spelling depends upon the adequacy of specific bonds and of specific hierarchies of bonds, all of which may be discussed under the general term "habits". . . . It is convenient to classify habits seen to be required for correct spelling as: habits of attending to syllables; habits of making appropriate perceptual attack upon new spelling problems; habits of making appropriate transfer from previously learned spellings.

Reed [43, p. 247], speaking also of habit formation, makes this statement:

The favorable effect of all these is apparently due to two elements in habit formation: the intensity of the impression and its frequency. Any device which increases these is helpful.

Jordan [27, p. 143] believes:

One intense experience of either pleasant or unpleasant nature may fix the correct spelling for all time.

Teacher direction brings with it increased attentiveness to the immediate task, in this case the word to be learned, while the use of the lantern means an opportunity for more intense perceptual impressions.

The results of the present study indicate that certain elements are more effective than others in the learning of spelling words by elementary school children. Certain minor points in method, however, must be determined by the conditions of the particular teaching situation. Time was saved in the last five-weeks' period of the present study by using the initial five-weeks' test in place of the weekly preliminary tests. This method freed all of the weekly time for the teaching and testing of words. The use of a preliminary test is a practical means of excusing children from the test who have the words of the week correctly spelled; in the present study it was also a necessary device for the accurate measurement of results.

A long-oral preliminary test, such as the one given in the present study, has certain advantages; it saves weekly time, as well as serving as a more thorough pre-test. The adequacy of an initial test to discover inaccuracy in word knowledge seems greater when the child has heard the word in an oral sentence than when he has also looked at the word before he is tested. This latter method is a half-learning which may result in temporary but not permanent recall. One of the real values of an initial test in the teacher-directed study method, which was the method found most successful in the present investigation, is that it reveals the difficulty of a particular group of words for a particular class. In the present study, the average child missed 35 per cent of the words in an eighty-word test. The procedure which proved to be most successful under these circumstances was to have all the children who missed words for the week study all the words missed under the teacher's direction. However, if a list of words were found to be very much easier for a particular class, some adaptation of method might prove to be more sensible.

A great deal has been said by the exponents of individual study in spelling of the amount of time that is wasted when an individual studies other words than the words he himself has misspelled. The present investigation does not bear out this belief, if conservation of time can be measured by results in learning. In the part of the study in which individuals used only their own word lists, the time used for study was the same, but the number of words correct on the final test was lower than they were when any other method was employed. It has been pointed out in the present chapter that this fact may be due in part to the inadequacy of initial tests as now used for the identification of unknown words. As it now stands, however, it would seem that there is a final gain in a group method of study, provided one is dealing with a correctly graded list of words.

This study has not attempted to solve the problem of the best distribution of review time. It has offered data on the value of directed reviews and home study as compared with no review. The results indicate that a distribution of time which gives 60 minutes a week to study of new words and 15 minutes a week to systematic review has 11 chances to 1 of giving better results than one which gives the whole 75 minutes to the study of new words. Such a distribution of time into four periods for new work and one for review gives the same mean number of words gained as does a method in which the five periods combined the study of the new words with the review of the words missed on Friday. This plan in which the time spent on the study of the new words is reduced from 75 minutes a week to 60 minutes a week with the additional 15 minutes spent on review is administratively advantageous since, over a long interval, review would interfere with scheduled spelling time on new words.

Of the methods experimented with, the plan of work for the week which seems to combine best the elements found to be statistically advantageous to the learning of words is this last one used:

Monday:

    Teach half of the new words for the week, using the lantern for presentation. Dictate the words just taught in a list and reteach the ones missed.

Tuesday:

    Teach the other half of the new words for the week, using the lantern for presentation. Dictate the words just taught in a list and reteach the ones missed.

Wednesday:

    Keep this day for systematic review of the back weeks' words.

Thursday:

    Dictate sentences using the new words of the week. Correct, using the lantern, and reteach the words missed.

Friday:

    Dictate the words for the week in a list. Correct with the lantern. Reteach the words missed.

The problem of this study has been to report and interpret the results of spelling teaching and learning so controlled as to give additional data on some of the problems in spelling method in which results previously published have been either conflicting or meagre. The problem of taking these commonly used methods, analyzing the elements in them, and so controlling their use that the effect might be measured has been carried on under normal schoolroom conditions. The results are essentially practical and adaptable to immediate use in the teaching of elementary school spelling.

BIBLIOGRAPHY

1. Archer, C. P. "Saving Time in Spelling Instruction." *J. Educ. Research*, Vol. 20, No. 2, pp. 122-132, September 1929.
2. Arps, G. F. "Work with Knowledge of Results vs. Work without Knowledge of Results." *Psychol. R. Monographs*, Vol. 28, No. 3, pp. 1-41, 1920.
3. Book, W. F. "How a Special Disability in Spelling Was Diagnosed and Corrected." *J. Applied Psychol.*, Vol. 13, No. 4, pp. 378-403, August 1929.
4. Book, W. F. and Harter, R. S. "Mistakes Which Pupils Make in Spelling." *J. Educ. Research*, Vol. 19, No. 2, pp. 106-118, February 1929.
5. Brandenburg, G. C. "The Spelling Ability of University Students." *Sch. and Soc.*, Vol. 7, No. 158, pp. 26-29, January 5, 1918.
6. Breed, Fred S. "A Plan for Teaching Spelling." *Ohio Schools*, Vol. 7, No. 8, pp. 301-302, October 1929.
7. Cornman, Oliver P. *Spelling in the Elementary School.* Ginn and Co., Boston, 1902. 98p.
8. Davis, Georgia. "Remedial Work in Spelling." *El. School J.*, Vol. XXVII, No. 8, pp. 615-626, April 1927.
9. *Department of Superintendence, Fourth Yearbook*, February 1926. Published by Department of Superintendence, National Association, Washington, D. C., pp. 126-172. 520p.
10. Devine, Verna G. and Hulten, C. E. "Pre-Testing and Spelling Ability." *El. English R.* Vol. 4, pp. 117-21, 1927.
11. Distad, H. W. and Davis, Eva M. "A Comparison of Column-Dictation and Sentence-Dictation Spelling with Respect to Acquisition of Meaning of Words." *J. Educ. Research*, Vol. 20, No. 5, pp. 352-360, December 1929.
12. Fulton, Martha J. "An Experiment in Teaching Spelling." *Ped. Sem.*, Vol. 21, No. 2, pp. 287-289, June 1914.
13. Garrett, Henry E. *Statistics in Psychology and Education.* Longmans, Green & Co., New York, 1926. 123p.
14. Garrison, S. C. and Garrison, K. C. *The Psychology of Elementary School Subjects*, Chaps. XVI-XVII, pp. 351-405. Johnson Publishing Co., 1929.
15. Gates, A. I. "A Test of Ability in the Pronunciation of Words." *T. C. Record*, Vol. XXVI, No. 3, pp. 205-219, November 1924.
16. Gates, A. I. *Psychology for Students of Education.* The Macmillan Company, New York, N. Y., 1923. xvi + 489p.
17. Gates, A. I. *Psychology of Reading and Spelling.* Contributions to Education, No. 129. Teachers College, Columbia University, New York, N. Y., 1922. vii + 108p.

18. GATES, A. I. and CHASE, ESTHER HEMKE. "Methods and Theories of Learning to Spell Tested by Studies of Deaf Children." *J. Educ. Psychol.*, Vol. XVII, No. 5, pp. 289-300, May 1926.

19. GREENE, HARRY A. "Syllabication as a Factor in Learning to Spell." *J. Educ. Research*, Vol. 8, No. 3, pp. 208-219, October 1923.

20. GUILER, W. S. "Validation of Methods of Testing Spelling." *J. Educ. Research*, Vol. 20, No. 3, pp. 181-190, October 1929.

21. HAWLEY, W. E. and GALLUP, JACKSON. "The 'List' versus the 'Sentence' Method of Teaching Spelling." *J. Educ. Research*, Vol. 5, No. 4, pp. 306-310, April 1922.

22. HEILMAN, J. D. *A Study in Spelling and Allied Problems.* Research Bulletin No. 2, State Teachers College of Colorado, 1919.

23. HOLLINGWORTH, LETA S. *The Psychology of Special Disability in Spelling.* Contributions to Education, No. 88, Teachers College, Columbia University, 1918. vi + 105p.

24. HORN, E. Principles of Method in Teaching Spelling, Derived from Scientific Investigations. *Eighteenth Yearbook N.S.S.E.*, Part II, Chap. III, pp. 52-77, 1919.

25. HUNKINS, R. V. "An Experiment in Column versus Dictation Spelling." *El. School J.*, Vol. 19, No. 9, pp. 689-699, May 1919.

26. IRMINA, MARY, SR. and Others. *Annotated Bibliography of Studies Relating to Spelling.* Catholic University of America Educational Research Bulletins, Vol. 3, No. 1. Catholic Education Press, Washington, D.C., 1928. 56p.

27. JORDAN, A. M. *Educational Psychology.* Henry Holt and Co., 1928. xiv + 460p.

28. KEENER, E. E. "Comparison of the Group and Individual Methods of Teaching Spelling." *J. Educ. Method*, Vol. 6, No. 1, pp. 31-35, September 1926.

29. *Keeping Pace with the Advancing Curriculum.* Research Bulletin of the National Education Association, Vol. III, Nos. 4-5. September-November, 1925. "Research in Spelling," pp. 138-141.

30. KILZER, L. R. "The Test-Study Method versus the Study-Test Method in Teaching Spelling." *School R.*, Vol. 34, No. 7, pp. 521-525, September 1926.

31. KINGSLEY, JOHN H. "The Test-Study Method versus the Study-Test Method in Spelling." *El. School J.*, Vol. 24, No. 2, pp. 126-129, October 1923.

32. LaRUE, DANIEL W. *The Child's Mind and the Common Branches.* The Macmillan Company, New York, 1924. x + 483p.

33. LAY, W. A. *Experimentelle Didaktik* (Third Edition, 1910), pp. 297-305; 351-370.

34. LESTER, JOHN A. "What Is a Misspelling?" *Sch. and Soc.*, Vol. 15, pp. 117-120, January 1922.

35. McCALL, W. A. *How to Experiment in Education.* The Macmillan Company, New York, 1926. 278p.

36. McKEE, PAUL. *Spelling Difficulty in Context Form.* Included in Master's Thesis. College of Education, State University of Iowa,

Iowa City, Iowa, 1921. p. 139. (Reported in *Fourth Yearbook*, Department of Superintendence.)

37. McKee, Paul. "Teaching Spelling by Column and Context Forms." *J. Educ. Research*, Vol. 15, Nos. 4-5, pp. 246-255, 339-348, April-May 1927.

38. Morton, R. L. "The Validity of Timed-Sentence and Column Tests in Spelling." *J. Educ. Research*, Vol. 5, pp. 444-447, May 1922.

39. Mossman, Lois Coffey. *Teaching and Learning in the Elementary School*. Houghton Mifflin Co., Boston, 1929. xv + 292p.

40. Nifenecker, Eugene A. *Reports on Some Measurements in Spelling in Schools of the Borough of Richmond*. Board of Education, New York, 1918.

41. Pearson, H. C. "Studies in Comparison of the Class Study and Independent Study Methods." *T. C. Record*, Vol. XIII, No. 1, pp. 49-66, January 1912.

42. Pearson and Suzzallo. *Essentials of Spelling*. American Book Co., New York, 1919. 196p.

43. Reed, Homer B. *Psychology of Elementary School Subjects*. Chap. XIV, pp. 224-272. Ginn and Co., 1927. 10 + 481p.

44. Schmidt, C. C. *Teaching and Learning the Common Branches*, Chap. IV, pp. 99-148. D. Appleton and Co., New York, 1929. xix + 418p.

45. Starch, Daniel. *Educational Psychology*. The Macmillan Company, New York, 1928. 536p.

46. Stigler, W. A. "Better Spelling and Less Drill." *Am. Childhood*, Vol. 14, pp. 25-27, April 1929.

47. Thorndike, E. L. "The Need of Fundamental Analysis of Methods of Teaching." *El. School J.*, Vol. 30, pp. 189-191, November 1929.

48. Tidyman, W. F. and Brown, Helen. "The Extent and Meaning of the Loss in 'Transfer' in Spelling." *El. School J.*, Vol. 18, No. 3, pp. 210-215, November 1917.

49. Tidyman, W. F. *The Teaching of Spelling*. World Book Co., Yonkers-on-Hudson, 1919. ix + 178p.

50. Watson, Alice E. *Experimental Studies in the Psychology and Pedagogy of Spelling*. Ms. dissertation, Teachers College, Columbia University. Vol. 1, pp. 1-245; Vol. 2, pp. 246-582. 1926.

51. Winch, W. H. "Additional Researches on Learning to Spell." *J. Educ. Psychol.*, Vol. 7, No. 1, pp. 93-110, January 1916.

52. Wolfe, H. A. and Breed, F. S. "Experimental Study of Syllabication." *Sch. and Soc.*, Vol. 15, No. 388, pp. 616-622, June 1922.

53. Woody, Clifford. "The Evaluation of Two Methods of Teaching Spelling." National Society of College Teachers of Education. *Fifteenth Yearbook*, 1926, pp. 155-171. University of Chicago Press, Chicago, Ill.

APPENDIX

TABLE I: TRAINING OF TEACHERS

TABLES II AND III: ACHIEVEMENT ON MENTAL AND STANDARDIZED TESTS OF CLASSES USED IN EXPERIMENTS

TABLE I

ACADEMIC TRAINING OF TEACHERS CONDUCTING THE TEACHING FOR THE SPELLING EXPERIMENTS

TEACHER NUMBER	TRAINING	No. OF YEARS' EXPERIENCE
1	Working for B.S.	7
2	B.S.	18
3	B.A.	14
4	B.S.	7
5	Working for B.S.	7
6	B.A.	6
7	B.S.	4
8	B.A.	7
9	B.S.	9
10	Working for B.S.	14
11	B.S.	5
12	Working for B.S.	10

TABLE II

RATING IN INTELLIGENCE AND ACHIEVEMENT TESTS OF SCHOOL GRADES IN WHICH EXPERIMENTAL TEACHING WAS CONDUCTED
SEPTEMBER 1928

| | NATIONAL GROUP | | | THORNDIKE-McCALL FORM I | | | | WOODY-McCALL FORM I | | | MORRISON-McCALL LIST 1 | | | |
| | INTELLIGENCE | | | GRADE | READING | | | ARITH-METIC | | | SPELLING | | | GRADE AVER-AGE |
	N.	Q1	Md Q3	Ed. Norm	Q1	Md	Q3	Q1	Md	Q3	Q1	Md	Q3	Md
3B	100	105–123–130		3.1	3.6	3.9	4.9	3.0	3.3	3.5	2.7	3.4	3.9	3.6
3A	100	99–107–127		3.6	4.1	4.5	5.3	3.5	3.8	4.0	3.0	3.5	4.2	4.2
4B	100	96–106–119		4.1	4.7	5.4	5.8	4.0	4.5	4.8	3.7	4.1	4.5	4.8
4A	100	102–108–118		4.6	4.9	5.7	6.6	4.3	4.9	5.3	4.1	5.1	5.4	5.0
5B	100	106–114–124		5.1	4.9	5.5	6.9	4.2	4.7	4.9	4.8	5.3	6.4	5.3
5A	100	102–118–134		5.6	6.6	7.4	10.5	5.2	5.6	6.3	5.3	6.1	6.5	6.6
6B	100	119–128–135		6.1	6.6	8.2	8.7	6.0	6.4	6.7	6.0	6.4	7.4	7.1

TABLE III

STANDING OF SCHOOL GRADES IN WHICH EXPERIMENTS WERE CONDUCTED IN INTELLIGENCE AND ACHIEVEMENT TESTS
JANUARY 1930

| | NATIONAL GROUP | | | | THORNDIKE-McCALL FORM 4 | | | | WOODY-FORM 3 | | | MORRISON-McCALL LIST 4 | | | GRADE AVER-AGE |
| | INTELLIGENCE | | | | READING | | | | ARITH-METIC | | | SPELLING | | | |
	Norm	Q1	Md	Q3	Norm	Q1	Md	Q3	Q1	Md	Q3	Q1	Md	Q3	Md
3B	100	102	109	116	2.9	3.1	4.2	4.7							
3A	100	108	112	122	3.4	4.0	4.7	5.1	3.5	3.7	4.3	3.1	3.4	4.1	4.1
4B	100	108	118	134	3.9	4.5	4.8	5.6	4.5	5.3	5.4	3.5	4.2	4.9	4.9
4A	100	115	120	129	4.4	4.7	5.6	6.5	5.2	5.4	6.0	4.1	4.7	5.2	5.6
5B	100	96	106	124	4.9	4.9	5.3	6.5	5.4	5.8	6.0	4.1	4.3	5.4	5.3
5A	100	104	113	122	5.4	5.1	5.8	6.3	5.3	5.8	6.0	4.2	4.9	6.3	5.6
6B	100	103	108	119	5.9	6.0	6.5	7.4	6.0	6.7	7.7	5.1	6.0	7.3	6.6
6A	100	108	115	132	6.4	6.0	6.8	7.4	6.2	6.7	7.7	5.5	6.3	7.7	6.8
7B	100	108	117	130	6.9	6.7	7.2	9.2	7.0	8.6	9.3	6.5	7.3	8.2	8.0
7A	100	118	126	136	7.4	7.4	10.2	13.3	6.8	8.3	9.1	7.3	8.0	10.5	8.8